AF577311

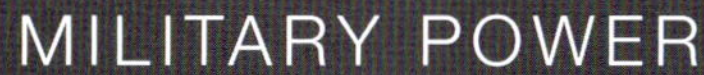

10TH MOUNTAIN DIVISION

FRED PUSHIES

First published in 2008 by Zenith Press, an imprint of MBI Publishing Company, 400 1st Avenue North, Suite 300, Minneapolis, MN 55401 USA.

Editor: Steve Gansen
Designer: Greg Nettles

Library of Congress Cataloging-in-Publication Data

Pushies, Fred J., 1952-
10th Mountain Division / Fred Pushies.
p. cm.
Includes index.
ISBN-13: 978-0-7603-3349-5 (pbk. : alk. paper)
ISBN-10: 0-7603-3349-1 (pbk. : alk. paper)
1. United States. Army. Mountain Division, 10th--History.
2. Mountain warfare--History. I. Title.
UD463.P87 2008
356'.1640973--dc22

2008020056

Printed in Singapore

On the cover: Private First Class Chris Smith, from the 87th Infantry Regiment, 10th Mountain Division, secures the perimeter during a patrol through Ameriya, a suburb of Baghdad, June 26, 2006. *Tech. Sgt. Jeremy T. Lock*

On the frontispiece: Two U.S. Army 2nd Battalion, 14th Infantry Regiment, 10th Mountain Division, Task Force Falcon, soldiers provide observation and radio communication security during a cordon-and-search operation in the towns of Tupaci and Jezero, Kosovo, Serbia. Task Force Falcon was the designation for the U.S. European Command (USEUCOM) forces assigned to the NATO-led peacekeeping Kosovo Force during Operation Joint Guardian. *Staff Sgt. Vincent A. King*

On the title page: A group of twelve 87th Mountain Infantry Regiment (reinforced) ski troopers, wearing winter camouflage uniforms and carrying knapsacks and rifles, stand near pine trees heavily covered with snow. *Denver Public Library, Western History Collection, Charles C. Bradley, TMD948*

On the back cover, top right: Soldiers from the 10th Mountain Division patrol Nuristan Province, Afghanistan, October 5, 2006. *Spc. Eric Jungels*

Bottom right: Soldiers of the 10th Mountain Division's 2nd Battalion, 87th Infantry Regiment, arrive for duty at a forward operating base in Afghanistan, March 6, 2006. *Sgt. 1st Class Michael Pintagro*

About the author:
Fred Pushies has spent the last seventeen years in the company of units assigned to U.S. Special Operations Command (SOCOM). He has skimmed across the waves with the SEALs in an eighty-two-foot-long Mark V Special Operations craft, flown at treetop level with the 160th Special Operations Aviation Regiment, and crunched through the brush with Force Recon Marines. His insight into America's elite combat soldiers is evident in his previous works, *Special Ops: America's Elite Forces in 21st Century Combat, 82nd Airborne, U.S. Air Force Special Ops, U.S. Army Special Forces, Marine Force Recon*, and *Weapons of the U.S. Navy SEALs.*

Contents

Chapter 1

ORIGINS

This portrait of David B. Allen shows him posing in his whites, or winter uniform, with his skis and poles crossed in front of him. He is crouching close to the ground and carrying a rifle and a knapsack with a white cover. Snow covers the ground, and Camp Hale barracks are in the background. *Denver Public Library, Western History Collection, David B. Allen, TMD757*

According to Gen. William Tecumseh Sherman, "War is hell," and it has grown more hellish over the years. While this fact has not diminished, the origin of the 10th Mountain Division can be directly traced to more recreational activities—skiing. In the fall of 1939, the German Blitzkrieg rumbled across Poland. Later the same year on November 30, the Russo-Finish War began as the Soviet Union, seeking to expand their empire, invaded Finland. In the United States, the thought that America would become involved in these conflicts grew stronger as, one by one, countries fell to these tyrannical despots.

Finland would eventually surrender to the Soviets four months later in the spring of 1940. Although they lost the war, the Finns made a valiant effort in defending their country. Through the employment of ski troops and guerilla tactics, the Finns cut supply lines, ambushed convoys, and attacked numerous Soviet troops. These soldiers wearing white camouflage and skis performed hit-and-run tactics and then swiftly and silently disappeared through the snow into the forest.

The initial successes of the Finnish Ski Troops and their tactics caught the attention of America's

Members of the 10th Mountain Division (left to right): Roger Langley, Charles Minot "Minnie" Dole, and Paul Lafferty pose outdoors at Camp Hale in Eagle County, Colorado. The American Alpine Club and National Ski Patrol were to be indispensable in the formation of the 10th Mountain Division. *Denver Public Library, Western History Collection, TMD436*

A member of an early training group that would later become the 10th Mountain Division stands on skis on Hurricane Ridge in the Olympic Range in Washington State. He is carrying a heavy pack, an M1 rifle, and ski poles. Mount Rainier can be seen in the distance. *Denver Public Library, Western History Collection, TMD408*

Assistant Secretary of War Louis Johnson. In January 1940, Secretary Johnson discussed the issue with Chief of Staff General Marshall, regarding the fielding of American troops trained and equipped for winter warfare, including equipment, supplies, transportation, and so forth. Three weeks later General Marshall advised Secretary Johnson that such operations were under consideration, noting the use of such force in the defense of the Alaskan territory.

Winter training was not necessarily a new concept, as soldiers stationed at Fort Snelling, Minnesota, conducted cold-weather training on an annual basis. General Marshall ramped up the training with the inclusion of tests and standardization of equipment essential to conducting military operations in a winter environment. A wide range of cold-weather gear from food to clothing was evaluated for use by soldiers in the field in severe-climate conditions.

The action of the Finnish Ski Troopers was not lost on those sportsmen in the ski and mountain community. The American Alpine Club urged the War Department to include mountain warfare training in the U.S. Army. Charles Minot "Minnie" Dole, president of the National Ski Patrol (NSP) committee, concurred. In the summer of 1940, Dole wrote to the president of the United States, Franklin D. Roosevelt "FDR", offering his help to recruit experienced skiers and train soldiers in this specialty. Dole pointed to the effectiveness of the Finnish Ski Patrols and the fact that in the United States there were some two million skiers. In his letter to FDR, he concluded, "It is more reasonable to make soldiers out of skiers, than skiers out of soldiers." The president referred the matter to the War Department.

Dole continued to press the issue, and in September 1940 he met with Chief of Staff Gen. George C. Marshall to present his ideas of an America Ski Patrol troop. By the fall of 1940, members of the America Alpine Club and the NSP were working with the army, using winter-warfare equipment and techniques. New equipment was developed and evaluated, including boots, down-filled sleeping bags, ropes, and even dehydrated foods. Over the coming months, the NSP would be instrumental in recruiting, screening, and evaluating civilian volunteers for duty with the army's ski patrol troops. By the summer of 1944, the association had recruited more than seven thousand sportsmen for the division.

The call went out, and ski patrol members, professional skiers, and mountaineers among both civilian and military units answered that call. The enlisted men recruited by the National Ski Association had considerable knowledge of civilian ski and mountain techniques but no military knowledge. Eventually, Capt. Rolf Monson, an Olympian, would lead the training of the first ski patrol unit, the 1st Division Patrol at Plattsburg Barracks, New York. Lieutenant John Woodward, an accomplished skier and former captain of the University of Washington ski team, entered active duty and was assigned to the 3rd Division

Two soldiers of the 10th Light Infantry Division ("Alpine"), which was later renamed the 10th Mountain Division, free climb a rock cliff on the obstacle course at Camp Hale in Eagle County, Colorado. The men wear wear uniforms, boots, gaiters, helmets, and packs, and have coiled ropes and rifles slung over their backs. An arrow pointing upward is painted on the rock. *Denver Public Library, Western History Collection, U.S. Army, TMD603*

A group of twelve 87th Mountain Infantry Regiment (reinforced) ski troopers, wearing winter camouflage uniforms and carrying knapsacks and rifles, stand near pine trees heavily covered with snow. *Denver Public Library, Western History Collection, Charles C. Bradley, TMD948*

Patrol at Fort Lewis. By the winter of 1940, members of the NSP were common visitors to the newly formed units, acting as advisers on techniques and equipment.

Winter Training

Members of the National Ski Association volunteered their expertise and served as instructors to U.S. Army, National Guard, and Army Reserve soldiers. The NSP, an organization within the association, had more than three thousand experienced skiers trained for work in the winter climate. These proficient skiers shared their skills with the fledgling soldiers, focusing on the familiarization, technical training, and use of ski equipment. While the soldiers were learning the skills from the NSP members, the NSP members were also learning, as they became acquainted with the northern areas of the United States. In the event the army had to call upon the NSP, they could serve as guides in these regions. With the prospect of war looming on the horizon, the War Department was not ready to fund a specialized force. The overall purpose of this exercise was not to form a dedicated ski patrol, but rather to lay the groundwork for future tactics, techniques, and procedures for missions in a winter environment.

Mountain Training

The next phase of training founded by the War Department was to establish training for troops in a mountainous environment. One primary concern centered on the success the German Army had in the Balkans, which involved the presence of armored forces and other troops specially trained for mountain operations. The G-3 (operations and training section) of the War Department recommended the construction of a high-mountain camp in December 1940. This recommendation would begin the construction of Camp Hale, which was located at Pando, Colorado, at an elevation of nine thousand feet above sea level. During this time, the 87th Mountain Infantry Battalion would be enlarged to a regiment at Fort Lewis, Washington. The expansion of the 10th Mountain Division gathered a number of experienced skiers and mountaineers from the NSP, as well soldiers transferred from various army units under the command of Lt. Col. Onslow S. Rolfe.

Although the men were coming together, the War Department did not have a definitive plan as to what to do with this newfound force. The directive for the formation of the mountain and ski troops was vague at best. How many troops were needed? How and where would they be deployed? Lieutenant Colonel Rolfe did not know whether his command was to develop a cadre of instructors or a viable force capable of combat. All of these issues became academic, when twenty-two days after the activation of the mountain unit, the Japanese carried out their surprise attack on Pearl Harbor. Ski troops were not initially at the top of the list for America's war planners.

Lieutenant Colonel Rolfe was left to his own devices, having no prior experience in mountain warfare. He had four officers subordinate to him who had some training in winter warfare and pack animals; however, none of them were experienced mountaineers or skilled handlers. The men recruited by the NSP were accomplished skiers and experienced mountaineers but lacked soldier skills.

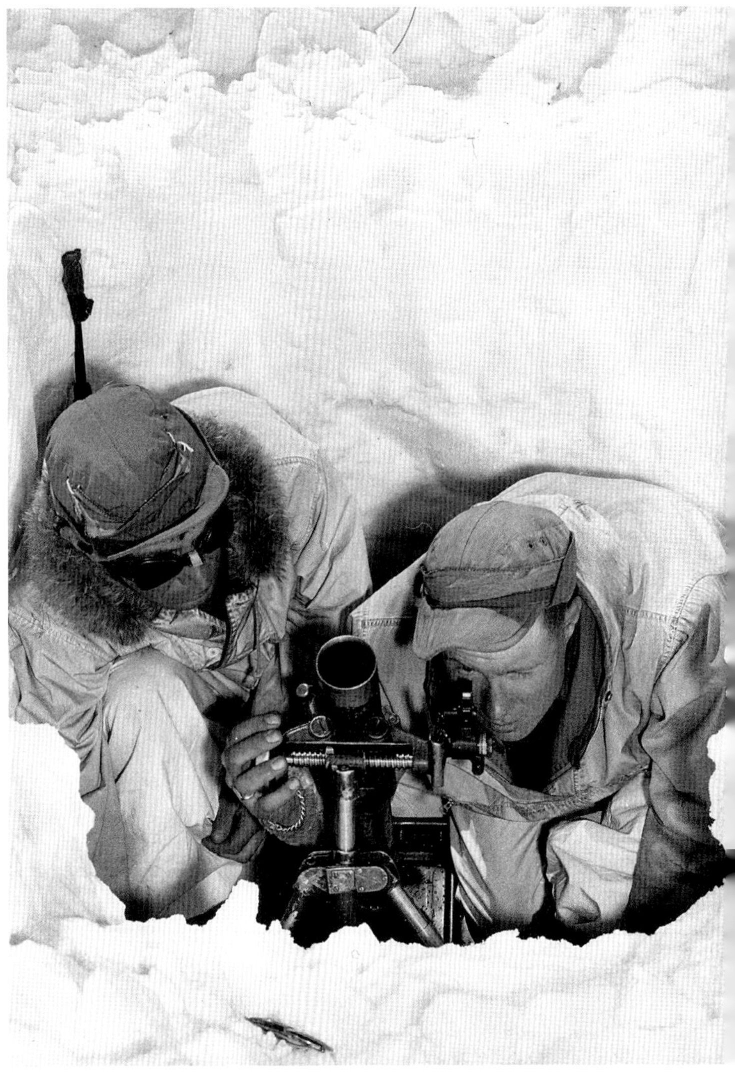

Two soldiers on maneuvers, members of Company G of the 86th Mountain Infantry Regiment, prepare to fire a practice round with 60mm mortar from Resolution Mountain in Eagle County, Colorado. The men, Thomas Boulson and Howard McDowell, huddle in a hole in the snow. McDowell sights the mortar. Both men wear winter gear and caps. Boulson wears snow goggles and has a fur-lined hood on his coat and a rifle on his back. *Denver Public Library, Western History Collection, U.S. Army, TMD636*

Camp Carson and Camp Hale

In September 1942, the Mountain Training Center was activated at Camp Carson, Colorado. In addition to the headquarters company being activated, there were pack artillery, signal, medical, quartermaster, engineer, ordnance, military police, antitank, and antiaircraft units. Two battalions of the 87th Mountain Infantry and an artillery battery from the 99th Field Artillery Battalion remained at Fort Lewis until they were relocated to Hunter Liggett Military Reservation, California, after two months. Their task was to carry out the evaluation of training techniques and procedures necessary for combat operations in a mountainous environment. In addition to the development of tactics, the unit would also test equipment and methods of transportation through mountains, dense forest, and primitive roadways.

In November 1942, the remainder of the Mountain Training Center relocated to Camp Hale. Ten days later on November 26, the 1st Battalion of the 86th Infantry was activated. In December 1942, the mountain troops that had conducted testing and evaluation moved to Camp Hale. The Mountain Training Center was at full strength and ready to begin training.

While the cadre from the Mountain Training Center were settling in at Camp Carson and Camp Hale, a detachment of ten officers and sixteen enlisted men were dispatched to Camp Edwards, Massachusetts, and then to Lincoln, New Hampshire. The mission of this detachment was to train selected members of the 36th Infantry Division in the basics of combat mountaineering.

Members of the 10th Light Division Alpine, or the 10th Mountain Division, march behind a Weasel snow-track (Snowcat) vehicle (an M29 cargo carrier) at Camp Hale. The driver of the vehicle wears goggles and a parka with the hood over his helmet. The vehicle is packed with gear, and the men wear parkas and carry packs, rifles, and snowshoes. *Denver Public Library, Western History Collection, U.S. Army, TMD613*

T15/M29 Weasel

The origins of the Weasel begin with an Englishman, Geoffrey Pike. At the onset of World War II, Pike concluded that 70 percent of Europe would be covered in snow for between 60 and 250 days that year. This brought about the need for a fast, lightweight vehicle capable of transporting men and equipment across the snowy fields of Europe. Charles Hunt, a World War II veteran of the 10th Mountain Division, relates, "At this time, there was no country that had a vehicle that could travel across snow."

Pike's concept was to create a vehicle that would travel over the snow rather than through it. Members of the British cabinet thought the idea had merit, but not enough to actually fund the project. Several months later Vice Adm. Lord Louis Mountbatten was made chief of combined operations and was tasked with ways to conduct offensive operations against the enemy. Pike had found an ally in Mountbatten and was soon assigned as the director of combined operations. His assignment was the invasion of Norway, codename Project Plough.

In April 1942, Mountbatten met with Prime Minister Winston Churchill and Gen. George C. Marshall to discuss the plan. At this time it was decided that an American company should be assigned to develop and manufacture Pike's "snow machine." Mr. Hunt describes Pike as "an eccentric fellow, rarely, if ever wore socks, and always wore flood pants, that is to say his trousers were a good six inches too short." Eventually, the project got pushed through, and in May 1942 the Studebaker Corporation in South Bend, Indiana, began to design, build, and evaluate the proposed vehicle.

Lieutenant Colonel Robert T. Frederick evaluated the concept and wrote a rather negative report to Gen. Dwight D. Eisenhower, discussing the shortcomings of the vehicle. Frederick concluded that due to the vulnerability of the vehicle and its lack of firepower, it could not be used in a full-scale assault but might be useful in reconnaissance patrols over hard snow–covered terrain. The report was not met with a favorable review by Eisenhower because he had already told the Allies that the project was in the works. As in so many circumstances, "politics" won out over common sense, and Ike pushed the project forward. As fate would dictate, Lieutenant Colonel Frederick would become the head of Project Plough and the snow machine. Subsequently the colonel would take command of a fledgling unit designated the First Special Service Force.

The Studebaker Corporation continued work on the snow machine, also known as the snow jeep; the official name would become the Weasel. As the war went on, the Weasel disappeared from the First Special Service Force, but it did find a home with the 10th Mountain Division. In July 1942, a group of soldiers from the 87th Infantry Mountain Regiment, forty enlisted men and five officers, were sent to British Columbia, Canada, to work on a secret project. Security was so tight that the men were not told their assignment until they reached Canada. A few weeks later, the Weasel arrived on site and the soldiers along with engineers from Studebaker began to test the new vehicle.

One of the major problems with the vehicle was that it would constantly throw a track. This meant the treads would slip off the wheels. The engineers designed an assortment of tracks, but the Weasel was notorious for throwing them off, one after the other. Mr Hunt related, "Eventually, they would go with a wider track, which tended to stay on the vehicle; this would be on the M29." All in all the men of the 87th spent five months testing the vehicle, eating good food, and getting in some skiing when they were off duty.

The early models were referred to as the T15, (*T* for test platform). As the program continued, the vehicle would be designated the T24/M24 and finally the M29. Worth noting is that the original design and concept called for the Weasel to be an expendable device and was even fitted with a location to place a TNT charge to destroy it. In the end it proved to be more valuable and the men grew to view it as a do-anything, go-anywhere type of vehicle. Albeit, it had its mechanical quirks, but like good old American soldiers, they loved to tinker with machines.

The Weasel was powered by a Studebaker 169 CID Champion automobile engine, which averaged thirty to thirty-five miles per hour on snow-covered terrain. Its overall length was ten feet six inches, and it could carry a payload of up to 1,200 pounds. The M29 could accommodate up to four soldiers—the driver and three passengers. The tracks on the M29 were twenty inches wide and rode on thirty-two bogie wheels. Later modifications included a pintle mount in the rear to accommodate a machine gun.

A soldier lies in a prone position and holds and sights a Browning automatic rifle during small-weapons practice at a range at Camp Swift in Bastrop County, Texas. The instructor, an army staff sergeant, holds a cigarette and looks on. Other soldiers sit or squat nearby. An ammunition clip and cartridge boxes are on the ground. *Denver Public Library, Western History Collection, U.S. Army, TMD617*

In July 1943, the 10th Light Division ("Alpine") was activated at Camp Hale. The division consisted of two new infantry regiments, one new pack artillery battalion, and one antiaircraft battalion. The division was under the command of Maj. Gen. Lloyd E. Jones. Most of the men came from the Mountain Training Center, which was deactivated with the creation of this new division.

Near the end of June 1944, the 10th Light Division relocated from Camp Hale, Colorado, to Camp Swift in Austin, Texas. Here, the soldiers received training on flat land. Rumors were rampant that the division would not deploy to Europe but rather head to Southeast Asia. When the soldiers were issued maps of Burma and given Japanese phrase books, the Southeast Asia deployment seemed probable. The men continued training, as rifle, artillery practice, and twenty-five-mile marches became part of the daily routine to build up the men's stamina.

Camp Swift would also take in some new tenants in early October; approximately six hundred mules arrived from Oklahoma joining those already in camp. The mules

Tenth Mountain Division soldiers learn how to tie boxes on the pack saddles of two mules at Camp Hale. Some of the soldiers are wearing steel helmets; others are wearing caps. The soldiers holding the mules' heads are wearing leather boots and jodhpurs. *Denver Public Library, Western History Collection, O'Rourke, TMD798*

would serve as pack animals transporting equipment for the mountain soldiers.

In October 1944, the commander of the 10th Light Division, General Jones, took ill and was replaced by Brig. Gen. George P. Hays. On November 6, 1944, the division was redesignated as the 10th Mountain Division. General Hays was promoted to major general and took command of the 10th at Camp Swift in November 1944. As a mountain division, the 10th was authorized to wear the blue-and-white "mountain" tab. General Hays was no stranger to combat; he had come to the 10th from the 2nd Division. In addition to his recent accomplishments, he was one of the few generals who had been awarded the Congressional Medal of Honor as a lieutenant during World War I.

A month later in the middle of December 1944, the 10th Mountain Division left Camp Swift, loaded up on troop ships, and embarked for Naples, Italy. The 86th was aboard the USS *Argentina*, while the 87th and 88th made their journey across the Atlantic aboard the USS *West Point*. The men of the 10th Mountain Division were going to war.

Chapter 2

HISTORY

Five 10th Mountain Division soldiers, members of the Company F, 86th Regiment, make preparations in the snow on Riva Ridge behind a screen of bushes. Four wear white coats and one wears a khaki coat. More mountain peaks are in the distance. *Denver Public Library, Western History Collection*

10th Mountain Division—World War II

With the Allied invasion on the beaches of Normandy, France, on June 6, 1944, combat in Italy was relegated to the background. For the soldiers of the 10th Mountain Division fighting in the Apennine Mountains, it was far from the "forgotten front." For the German army as well, the battles in the Italian Alps were as real and lethal as those their comrades were facing in France. During the campaign the mountain soldiers of the 10th would do battle with nine German divisions that were well entrenched and occupying the high ground. By the end of the campaign, five of the nine German divisions would be totally destroyed as effective combat units. The men of the 10th Mountain Division not only had to fight the Germans, but also had to deal with the elements and environment—the jagged mountains, cliffs, rivers, lakes, and towns. In early January 1945, the 86th Infantry Regiment arrived at the frontlines near Mount Belvedere in the North Apennine Mountains of Italy.

By January 20, 1945, all three regiments of the 10th had arrived in Italy and were positioned along the Serchio Valley

During the air preparation of the big "push" in Italy by the U.S. Fifth Army, the men, mules, and armor of the 10th Mountain Division and supporting tank units move forward between 0830 and 0910 hours on April 14, 1945, in Bologna, Italy. *U.S. Army photo*

RIVA RIDGE BATTLE DIAGRAM

February 18 – 25

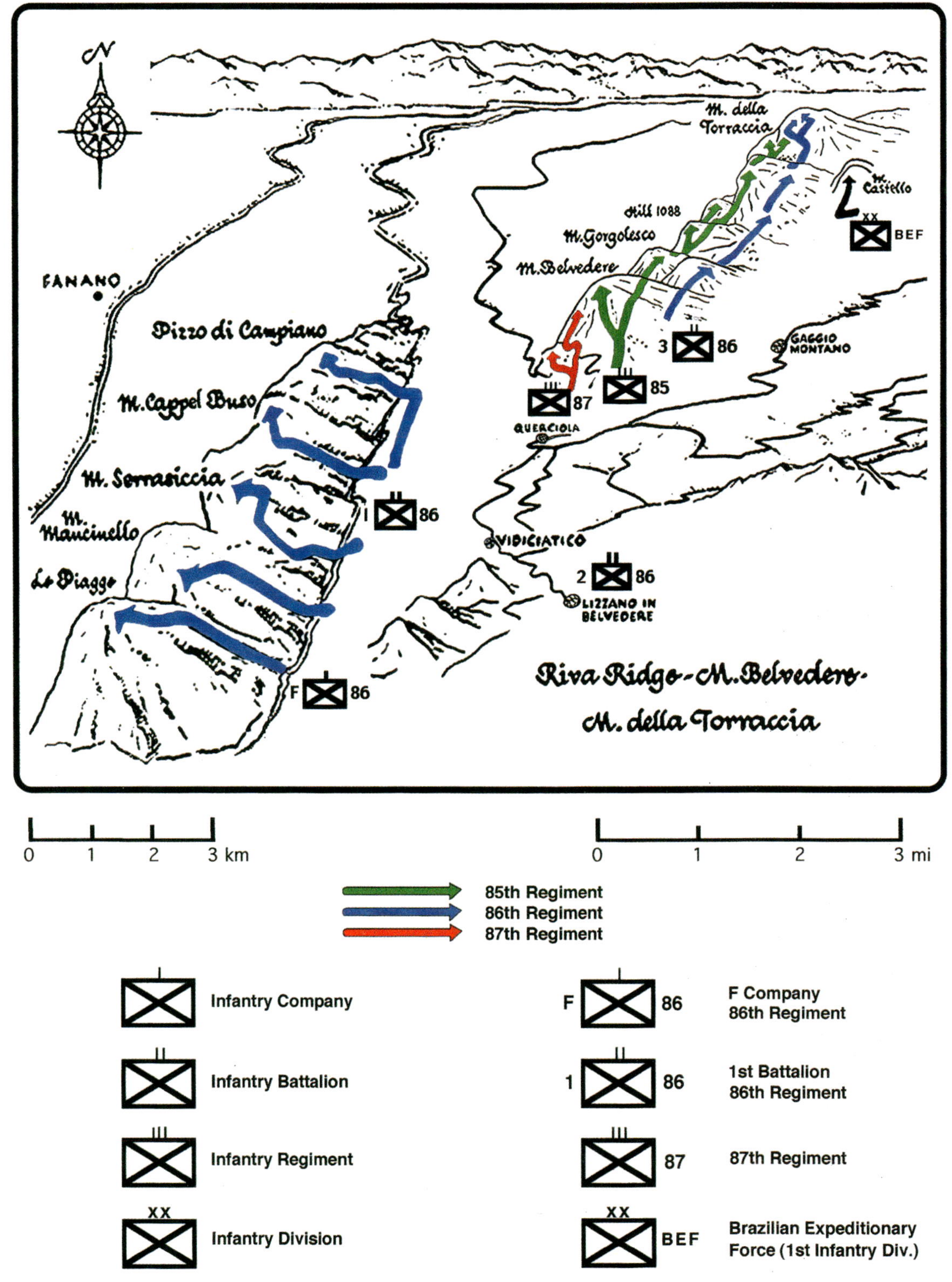

Courtesy of John Imbrie and Thomas Brooks, 10th Mountain Division Association

ATTACK ON RIVA RIDGE

February 18 - 25

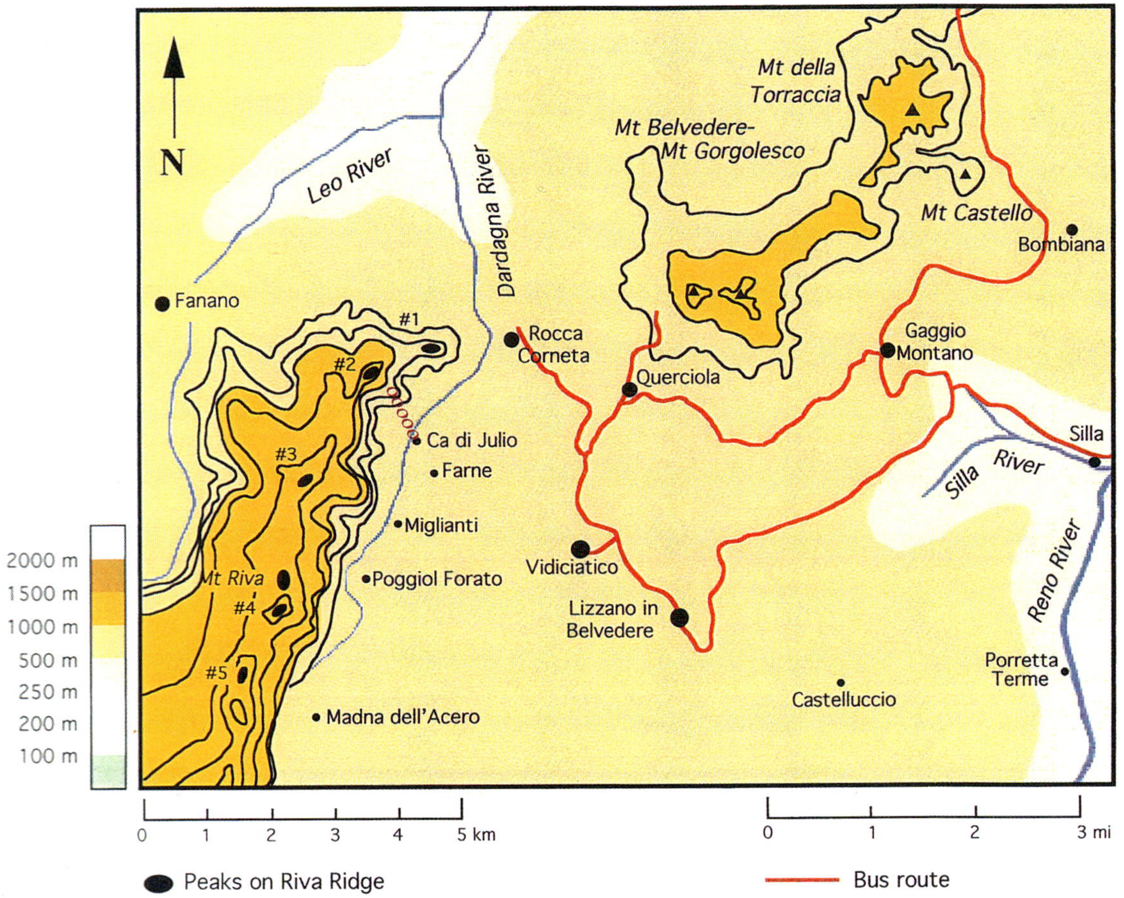

ooooo Aerial tramway constructed by Company D,126th Mountain Engineers. The tramway was 1700 ft long and terminated on a shoulder of Mt. Cappel Buso at an elevation of 2625 ft.

The lowest contour traced on Riva Ridge is 800 meters.
The lowest contour traced on the Mt Belvedere-Mt della Torraccia Ridge is 900 meters.

ATTACK ON RIVA RIDGE

OBJECTIVE	ELEVATION	COMPANY	DEPARTURE POINT
#1. Pizzo di Campiano	3156 ft	86-A 2nd Platoon	Ca di Julio
#2. Mt Cappel Buso	3776 ft	86-B	Pianacci
#3. Mt Serrasiccia	4577 ft	86-C	Miglianti
Mt Riva	4626 ft		
#4. Mt Mancinello	4764 ft	86-A 1st,3rd,4th Platoons	Poggiol Forato
#5. Le Piagge	4859 ft	86-F	Madna dell'Acero

Note: Elements of 86-D accompanied 86-B and 86-C.

← 9 miles →

Courtesy of John Imbrie and Thomas Brooks, 10th Mountain Division Association

Soldiers of the 10th Mountain Division pass by Nazi soldiers as they move on toward their next objective. Tank destroyers, which had been attached to the division as they pressed their attack in the Italian Alps, can be seen in the background. *U.S. Army photo*

and Mount Belvedere. The 85th was commanded by Col. Raymond Barlow, the 86th by Col. Clarence Tomlinson, and the 87th by Col. David Fowler. Here, the division was up against the German positions that were positioned along the five-mile-long Mount Belvedere–Monte della Torraccia Ridge. General Lucian Truscott Jr., who had just taken command of the Fifth Army, informed General Hays of his strategy for dealing with the enemy. The plan called for the 10th to first capture Mount Belvedere, which served as an enemy observation post. The artillery observation post provided the Germans with a view of Highway 65, which was one of the main routes into the Po Valley. Protecting Mount Belvedere were more Germans on Riva Ridge toward the west.

In order to capture Mount Belvedere, the division would first have to assault Riva Ridge. Riva was a codename for the ridge that, from north to south, included the peaks Pizzo di Campiano, Mount Cappel Buso, Mount Serrasiccia, Mount Riva, Mount Mancinello, and Le Piagge. The 1st Battalion and Company F, 2nd Battalion, 86th Mountain Infantry, conducted the assault on Riva Ridge, which was a sheer mountain face that required the soldiers to make a vertical assent of nearly two thousand

A machine gunner and two riflemen of Company K, 87th Mountain Infantry, 10th Mountain Division, cover an assault squad routing Germans out of a building in the background. March 4, 1945. Porretta-Moderna Highway. Sassomolare area, Italy. *U.S. Army photo*

feet. The Germans believed that the cliffs were not scalable and so had manned the mountaintop with only one battalion of soldiers. The mountain soldiers of the 10th were the ones who were tasked to make the assault. Riva Ridge was to the 10th Mountain what Pointe du Hoc was to the U.S. Rangers.

Harry Coleman, an infantryman with the 10th in Italy, related his part in this pivotal battle:

> Headquarters expected a lot of casualties. Normally, we had one medic; for this operation we had five or six. I was carrying a BAR (Browning automatic rifle), which was almost as big as I was. My first sergeant, Ed Thivridge, took the BAR away from me and gave me an M1 to carry in its place. We arrived on the night of February 17 and were trucked down to a staging area, where we took over a farmhouse at the foot of the ridge. They told us that nobody was to leave the house. If we had to use the outhouse, we had to put on the farmer's coat. When it came time for us to head up the mountain, we were ordered to remove all the ammunition from our guns. We were told to put the

ammo in our pockets and keep it handy. The commander did not want to take the chance of an accidental discharge, which would have alerted the enemy. General Hayes told the men, 'Stay in touch with the man in front of you and we'll all meet at the top.' Seven hundred men converged on Riva and began the hard climb under the cover of darkness. There were no ropes or pitons; we did it the hard way. I pushed the guy in front of me and pulled the guy behind me.

After a great deal of scouting, it was determined the assault would be at night, and on February 18, 1945, the soldiers of the 86th began their climb. The attack caught the Germans by surprise, enabling the mountain infantrymen a complete success.

After the successful attack on Riva by the 86th, Mount Belvedere was the next to be assaulted. Mount Belvedere was heavily manned and protected by minefields. On February 19, soldiers of the 85th and 87th regiments fixed bayonets and began their assault on Mount Belvedere. As had been the case on Riva, the mountain soldiers took the enemy by surprise. The attack was hard fought, but they captured the mountaintop. The Germans mounted several counterattacks over the next two days but were unable to retake the valuable real estate. With the successful capture of Mount Belvedere, the 10th was in a position to breach the German's Apennine Mountain line, take Highway 64, and open the way to the Po Valley. On April 14, 1945, the final phase of the war in Italy began as the Fifth Army drove

Soldiers of the 87th Mountain Regiment take another Italian village and are aided by Sherman tanks of the Fifth Army. *U.S. Army photo*

toward the Po Valley with the 10th Mountain Division spearheading the force.

On April 20, 1945, lead elements of the 85th Infantry Regiment of the 10th Mountain Division were the first American units to break out into the Po Valley. Joining the 10th in an ad hoc task force would be tanks and tank destroyers. Task Force Duff, commanded by Brig. Gen. Robinson Duff, drove north to the Po River. As the unit advanced through the valley, the soldiers had to battle through several strategic German positions, including trenches and foxholes, and they endured fighting in the towns and villages. The task force continued to press their attack even though both of their flanks were exposed. By nightfall, Task Force Duff had captured the bridge crossing the Panaro River at Bomporto. On the morning of April 23, the 10th was the first division to reach the Po River. The 1st Battalion of the 87th Mountain Infantry, the original mountain infantry unit, made the crossing in fifty lightweight canvas boats while under enemy fire. By the end of the day on April 25, all elements of the task force had crossed the Po River.

Lieutenant General Von Senger, commander of the 14 Panzer Corps, told General Hays that the 10th had completely broken through two panzer corps, forcing

In the Monte Grande area of Italy, an infantryman of the 86th Mountain Regiment takes a well-earned break after climbing and fighting in the mountains. February 22, 1945. *U.S. Army photo*

Medal of Honor Recipient—10th Mountain Division

JOHN D. MAGRATH (Posthumous)

Rank and organization: Private First Class, U.S. Army, Company G, 85th Infantry, 10th Mountain Division. Place and date: Near Castel d'Aiano, Italy, April 14, 1945. Entered service at: East Norwalk, Conn. Birth: East Norwalk, Conn. G.O. No.: 71, July 17, 1946. Citation: He displayed conspicuous gallantry and intrepidity above and beyond the call of duty when his company was pinned down by heavy artillery, mortar, and small-arms fire near Castel d'Aiano, Italy. Volunteering to act as a scout and armed with only a rifle, he charged headlong into withering fire, killing two Germans and wounding three in order to capture a machine gun. Carrying this enemy weapon across an open field through heavy fire, he neutralized two more machine-gun nests. He then circled behind four other Germans, killing them with a burst as they were firing on his company. Spotting another dangerous enemy position to his right, he knelt with the machine gun in his arms and exchanged fire with the Germans until he had killed two and wounded three. The enemy now poured increased mortar and artillery fire on the company's newly won position. Private First Class Magrath fearlessly volunteered again to brave the shelling in order to collect a report of casualties. Heroically carrying out this task, he made the supreme sacrifice—a climax to the valor and courage that are in keeping with highest traditions of the military service.

PO VALLEY SOUTH: BATTLE DIAGRAM

April 20 – 22

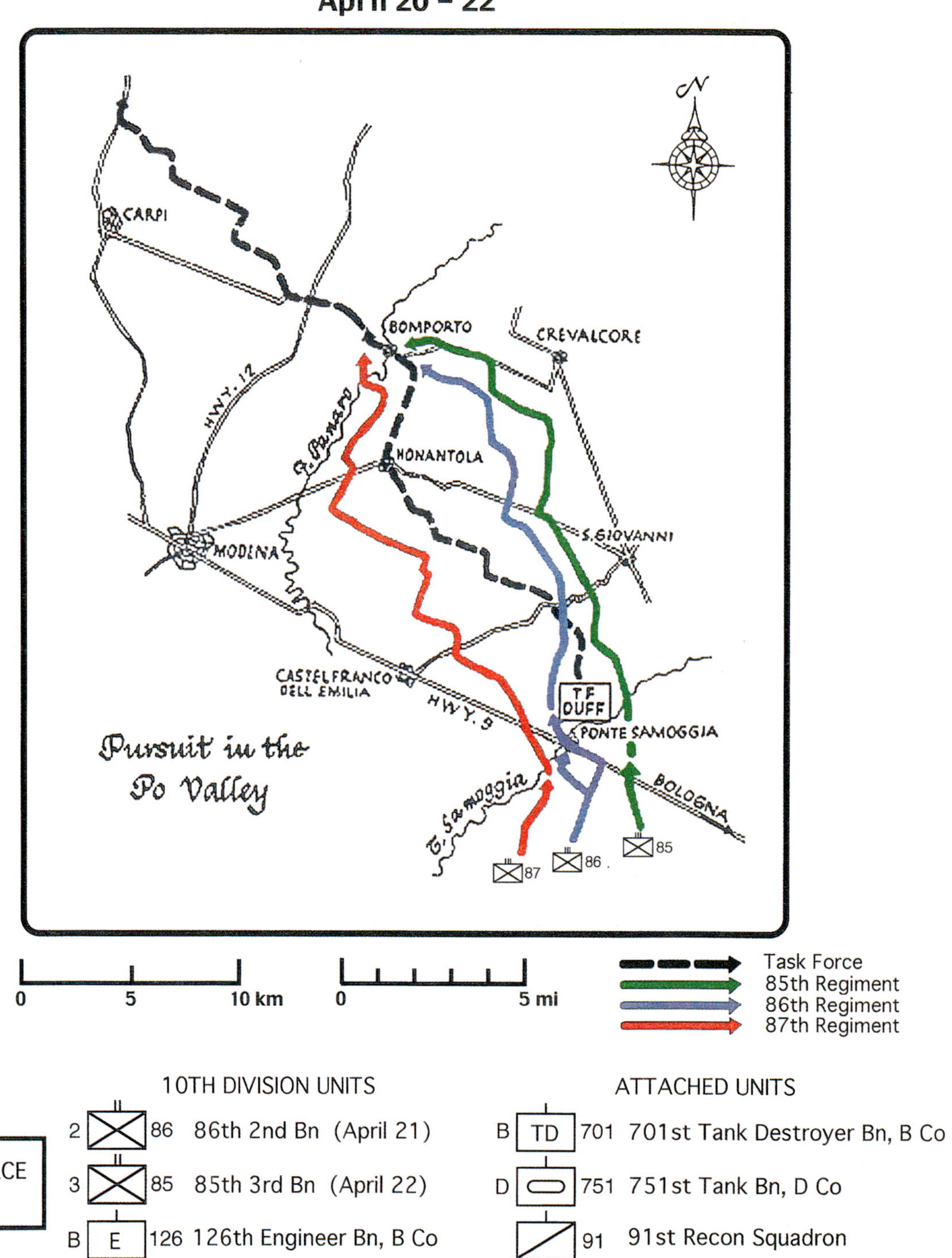

Courtesy of John Imbrie and Thomas Brooks, 10th Mountain Division Association

PO RIVER CROSSING
April 23 – 24

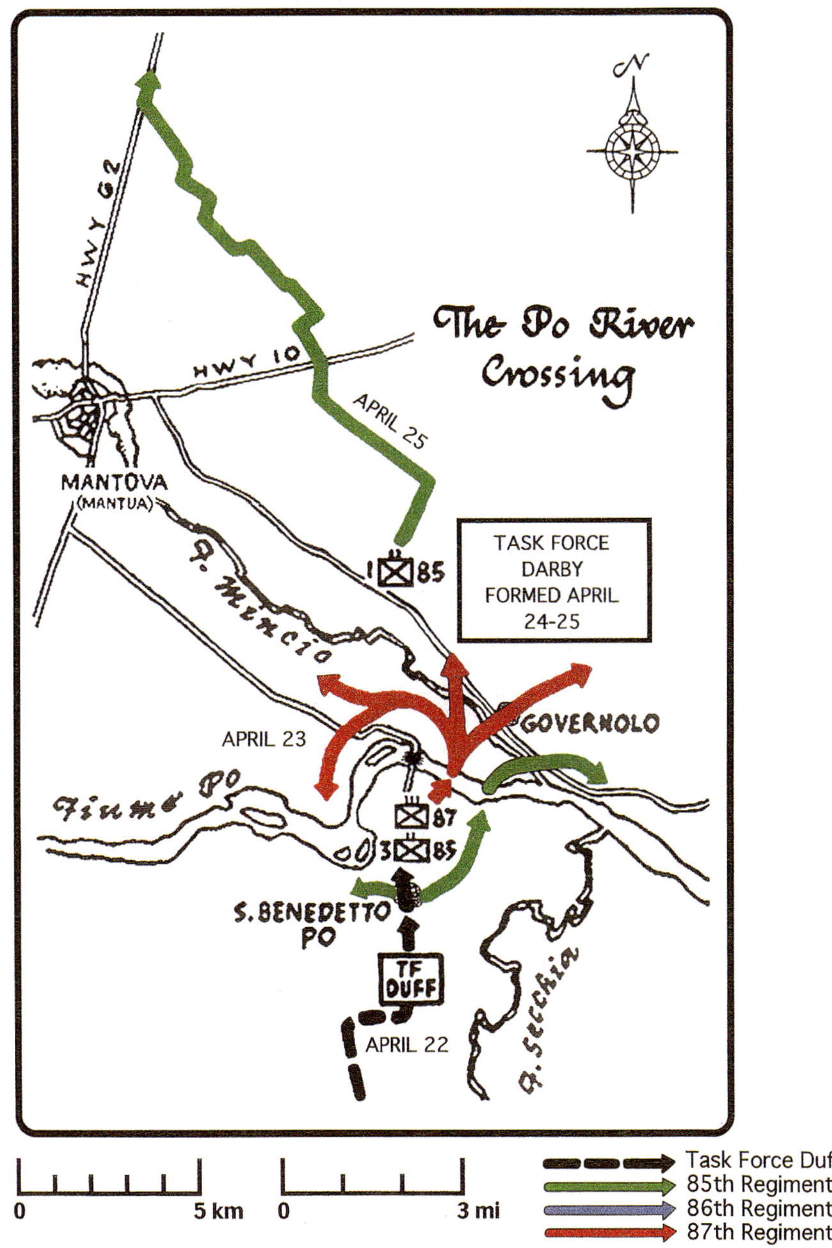

The first crossing, under fire, was made at noon on 23 April by 87th 1st Battalion. By early evening, 85th 3rd Battalion and the rest of the 87th were across, quickly followed by the rest of the 85th. By the evening of the 24th, the entire 86th Regiment was across, ready to join Task Force Darby, which struck out for Villafranca at 6:00 pm on the 25th, following a route scouted earlier that day by 85th 1st Battalion.

Courtesy of John Imbrie and Thomas Brooks, 10th Mountain Division Association

Field artillerymen man a 57mm cannon. This gun crew is firing in support of the 88th Division troops crossing the Po River in Italy. *U.S. Army photo*

Von Senger, his staff, and many of his soldiers into the cold water of the Po River. During his surrender Von Senger said the 10th Mountain Division had proven to be a most worthy adversary.

The final combat for the 10th Division took place in the vicinity of Lake Garda, a canyon lake at the foothills of the Alps. On April 25, the 1st Battalion of the 85th Infantry Regiment moved out toward an airport near the town of Villafranca di Verona. As the 85th headed out toward their target, another task force, Task Force Darby, headed out with orders to capture the town of Verona, located ten miles northeast of Villafranca. The task force, commanded by Col. William Darby, consisted of the 86th Infantry Regiment, three tank battalions, a battalion of field artillery, and a handful of engineers. By the end of the day, Task Force Darby had achieved its objectives and linked up with the 85th.

On April 27, 1945, the first troops reached the south end of Lake Garda, cutting off the German army's main escape route to the Brenner Pass. As the 10th pressed their attacks, they were met with challenges because the German had destroyed several tunnels and created roadblocks. Undaunted by the enemy's delaying tactics, the 10th used DUKWs (six-wheeled amphobious trucks),

German prisoners of war who were captured during the battle for Monte Terminale, Italy, are marched to the rear. There they will be questioned and interned. The soldiers are most likely members of the Mittenwald battalion of crack German mountain troops. *U.S. Army photo*

the obstacles were bypassed, and the towns of Riva and Tarbole at the head of the lake were captured. On May 2, 1945, any sign of organized resistance had ended, and the German army in Italy surrendered. Five days later, Germany surrendered to the Allied forces.

On May 20, 1945, the 10th relocated to northeastern Italy, to Udine, where they linked up with troops from the British 8th Army. Their new mission was to prevent any western movement by Yugoslavian forces under the command of General Tito. Harry Coleman related an incident in which a Yugoslavian tank rolled up to a schoolhouse in the area. The tank edged nearer and nearer until the large cannon was dangerously close to the building. There was no guessing what the tank commander had in mind. One of the 10th's officers approached the vehicle and had a talk with the tank commander. Shortly thereafter, the tank withdrew and drove away, without firing a shot.

In July 1945, the 10th was ordered back to the states to begin training and preparation for the invasion of Japan. As the mountain soldiers traveled across the Atlantic, they heard about the atomic bomb drop on Hiroshima, Japan. The 10th Mountain Division would not be going to the Pacific. Japan surrendered on August 15, 1945. By September, the 10th was back home after

Engineers construct a pontoon bridge over the violent Arno River under extreme conditions. The efforts of the combat engineers provide a gateway further inland to press the attack on the Germans. *U.S. Army photo*

a thirty-day furlough, and on November 30, 1945, the 10th Mountain Division was deactivated.

Postwar Missions

After World War II, the veterans of the 10th Mountain Division went back to their origins—skiing and mountaineering. With the war behind them, many Americans became active in these outdoor activities. Members of the 10th played a large role in turning skiing into a big name sport and popular vacation industry. Soldiers who had served in the 10th laid out ski hills, built ski lodges, designed ski lifts, and improved ski equipment. Some of these men started ski magazines and opened ski schools. Vail, Aspen, Sugarbush, Crystal Mountain, and Whiteface Mountain are but a few of the ski resorts built by 10th Mountain veterans.

10th Infantry Division in the Cold War

The 10th was reactivated at Fort Riley, Kansas, as a training division on July 1, 1948. As a training unit, the 10th would not retain the wartime designation as a Mountain Division and lost the mountain tab as a result. The division had the

Supported from the air by fighter-bombers, 10th Mountain Division men on the Porretta Moderna Highway in Della Vedetta, Italy, fire on Germans about two hundred yards away. *U.S. Army photo*

mission of processing and training new soldiers for service with other army units. The outbreak of the Korean Conflict in June 1950 expanded the division's training mission. The 10th would conduct basic training for 123,000 soldiers from 1948 to 1953. In May 1954, the 10th Training Division was deactivated and became the 10th Infantry Division. The new division would be sent to Europe, replacing the 1st Infantry Division in Germany. With its headquarters in Wurzburg, all of its component units were positioned in a seventy-five-mile radius. This arc went from Frankfurt to Nuremberg, which was the central position of the North Atlantic Treaty Organization (NATO) defense forces. The 10th Infantry Division consisted of nine infantry battalions, four artillery battalions, and one tank battalion. This formidable force was at the hub of action as America waged the Cold War. In 1958, the 10th's tour in Europe was over, and they were replaced by the 3rd Infantry Division. The 10th Infantry Division was sent to Fort Benning, Georgia, where it was deactivated on June 14, 1958.

On February 13, 1985, the 10th Mountain Division (Light Infantry) was officially reactivated, at Fort Drum, New York.

Infantrymen of the 10th Mountain and soldiers from the Fifth Army maneuver down the winding roads of the mountain of Monte Grande in Italy. In addition to the trucks, a group of Weasels can be seen in the background. *U.S. Army photo*

An M998 high-mobility multipurpose wheeled vehicle (HMMWV) comes down the ramp to the front entrance of an U.S. Air Force C-5B Galaxy cargo plane. The U.S. Army personnel connected to the HMMWV are from Company B, 187th, and HQ 222nd of the 10th Mountain Division, Fort Drum, New York. They arrived at Mogadishu Airport to reinforce the small contingent of U.S. personnel deployed to Somalia in support of Operation Restore Hope. A soldier sits atop the HMMWV manning a 40mm Mk 19 grenade launcher. *Sgt. M. Preston*

Two U.S. Army troops from the 10th Mountain Division are shown conducting a nighttime sweep for weapons in the small Somali village of Afgooye. Some Somali men, women, and children are seen at the right. The 10th Mountain Division from Fort Drum, New York, is deployed to Somalia as part of Operation Restore Hope. *Master Chief Photographer's Mate Terry Mitchell*

As stated on GlobalSecurity.org: "The 10th was the first division of any kind formed by the army since 1975 and the first based in the northeast United States since World War II. The 10th Mountain Division was designed to meet a wide range of worldwide infantry-intensive contingency missions. Equipment design was oriented toward reduced size and weight for reasons of both strategic and tactical mobility."

Operation Restore Hope—Somalia

On December 3, 1993, the division headquarters was designated as the headquarters for all army forces (ARFOR) of the Unified Task Force (UNITAF) for Operation Restore Hope. The division's mission was to secure major cities and roads to provide safe passage of relief supplies to the starving Somali population. Due to 10th Mountain Division efforts, humanitarian agencies declared an end to the food emergency, and factional fighting decreased. As part of Operation Continue Hope (May 1993 through March 1994) the United Nations (UN) assumed the task of securing the flow of relief supplies in Somalia. All remaining division units in Somalia came under the control of a new headquarters, United Nations

Right-side profile shot of a U.S. Army UH-60 Black Hawk helicopter on the ground at Merca, Somalia. Five soldiers from the 2nd Brigade, 10th Mountain Division, Fort Drum, New York, jump out of the helicopter for the air assault into Merca from Baledogle, Somalia, on December 31, 1992. This mission is in direct support of Operation Restore Hope. *Sgt. Jeffrey Brady*

Army troops from the 10th Mountain Division, Fort Drum, New York, are escorted to their helicopters by a safety officer during air assault rehearsal on the flight deck of the nuclear-powered aircraft carrier USS *Dwight D. Eisenhower* (CVN-69) en route to Haiti. *PH3 Russell*

Operations in Somalia (UNOSOM II). It was during this time that the ill-fated mission of Task Force Ranger would take place.

On October 3, 1993, Special Operations Task Force Ranger (TFR) conducted a daylight raid on an enemy stronghold, deep in militia-held Mogadishu. Operators from Delta Force had successfully captured some of warlord Mohammed Farah Aidid's key aides while members of the 75th Ranger Regiment provided security for the Delta teams. Although the Delta operators successfully completed their task, the mission went south after one of the 160th Special Operations Aviation Regiment helicopters was shot down. It became even more intense after the second MH-60 was taken down by a rocket-propelled grenade (RPG). The mission quickly shifted to a rescue operation to get to the downed Black Hawk helicopters and extract their crews.

Many hours of intense fighting continued as the beleaguered members of TFR were surrounded by hundreds of Somali gunmen. The call was made to the quick reaction force (QRF) to mount a rescue. The 2nd Battalion, 14th Infantry (2/14th Infantry) QRF was dispatched to secure the ground evacuation route. In addition to the 10th Mountain soldiers, there were two Malaysian mechanized companies with armored personnel carriers (APC) and one Pakistani tank platoon. As darkness fell, the 2/14th Infantry was reinforced with coalition armor, and for three hours they fought a moving gun battle from the gates of the port to the Olympic Hotel and the Ranger perimeter. The 2/14th was successful in linking up with the Rangers and began withdrawal under fire along a route secured by Pakistani forces. As dawn broke over the city, the exhausted soldiers made their way back to the protective Pakistani compound at the city's stadium. Task Force Ranger suffered nineteen killed in action (KIA) and fifty-seven wounded. The 2/14th had one killed and twenty-nine wounded. On March 12, 1994, the soldiers of the 10th returned to Fort Drum.

Operation Uphold Democracy—Haiti

The 10th Mountain Division served as the nucleus of the Multinational Force Haiti (MNF Haiti) and Joint Task Force 190 (JTF 190) in Haiti during Operation Uphold Democracy. The MNF Haiti was the U.S.-led coalition force in Haiti that included soldiers from twenty

A convoy of 10th Mountain Division troops drive down a street near the Port-au-Prince Airport during Operation Uphold Democracy. Helicopters line the sky in the background. *Spc. Michael J. Halgren*

Soldiers of Company B, 2nd Battalion, 87th Infantry, 10th Mountain Division, armed with M16 A2 rifles and M249 squad automatic weapons (SAW), climb an outside staircase to raid a building in Cap Haitian. The facility was suspected of containing a cache of weapons. U.S. military troops are in Haiti to preserve law and order and to restore the democratic government. *Spc. Jean-Marc Schaible*

U.S. Army Private First Class Malala Salu (left) is armed with an M16 rifle. As part of Company C, 2nd Battalion, 14th Infantry, 10th Mountain Division, he pulls security while UH-60 Black Hawk helicopters, which transported the soldiers, depart. This air assault is part of the training the soldiers from Company C will receive at Camp McGovern in Bosnia-Herzegovina. The soldiers will also learn about the mission of Task Force 1/77 (1st Battalion, 77th Armor), which is force protection and setting up a temporary checkpoint during Operation Joint Guardian. *Spc. Tracey L. Hall-Leahy*

A U.S. Army soldier wears a night vision device on his helmet while on night patrol in Eagle Base, Tuzla, Bosnia-Herzegovina. The soldier is part of the 2nd Battalion, 14th Infantry, 2nd Brigade, 10th Mountain Division (Light Infantry) taking part in Operation Joint Guardian. *Spc. Cory Montgomery*

nations. At 0930 hours, on September 19, 1994, the division's 1st Brigade conducted the army's first air assault from an aircraft carrier. This force consisted of fifty-four helicopters and almost two thousand soldiers. They occupied the Port-au-Prince Airport. This was the largest army air operation conducted from a carrier since the Doolittle Raid in World War II, where U.S. Army Air Force bombers were launched off of a carrier to attack Tokyo.

The division's mission was to create a secure and stable environment to allow the legitimate government of Haitian president Jean-Bertrand Aristide to be reestablished and democratic elections to be held. The final step in preparing for Aristide's return from exile occurred early on October 13, when General Cedras, his family, and members of his de facto government left the country for Panama. When President Aristide returned to the Port-au-Prince Airport on October 15, 1994, his security was provided courtesy of the 10th Mountain Division. On January 15, 1995, the 10th Mountain Division handed over control of the MNF Haiti to the 25th Infantry Division and headed home.

Operation Joint Guardian—Bosnia

The 642nd Engineer Company deployed for Bosnia on March 18, 1997, for a six-month tour constructing and maintaining roads and base camps. Two companies of the 2nd Battalion, 14th Infantry, deployed for Bosnia a day later. Company B's mission was to defend a critical bridge site; Company C's mission was to act as the theater reserve.

Task Force Eagle

In the fall of 1998, the 10th received notice that it would be serving as the senior headquarters of Task Force Eagle. Their mission was to provide a peacekeeping force to support the ongoing operation

Two U.S. Army 2nd Battalion, 14th Infantry Regiment, 10th Mountain Division, Task Force Falcon soldiers provide observation and radio communication security during a cordon and search operation in the towns of Tupaci and Jezero, Kosovo, Serbia. Task Force Falcon is the designation for the U.S. European Command (USEUCOM) forces assigned to the NATO-led peacekeeping Kosovo Force during Operation Joint Guardian. *Staff Sgt. Vincent A. King*

within the multinational division–north of responsibility in Bosnia and Herzegovina. The division staff began preparation for Stabilization Force Six (SFOR6). The division would be split into two operations: Task Force Drum for those soldiers remaining in the north and Task Force Eagle for those to be deployed to Bosnia.

In preparation for the Bosnia assignment, four major events were staged in 1999, including an SFOR6 conference in Tuzla, Bosnia; a deployment exercise at Fort Drum as a rehearsal; a conference at Fort Drum and Fort Hood; and an inter-theater rehearsal by some staff members, with other units in Bosnia. Select division units began deploying in late summer to link up with their commander, Maj. Gen. James Campbell, who had preceded his soldiers to Bosnia.

After successfully performing their mission in Bosnia, the division units conducted a transfer of authority, relinquishing their assignments to soldiers of the 49th Armored Division, Texas National Guard. By early summer 2000, all 10th Mountain Division soldiers had returned safely to Fort Drum. After conducting humanitarian, training, and operational deployments together, the 10th Mountain Division had earned the distinction of being the most deployed army division during the 1990s, a period that saw the greatest number of missions for U.S. military forces, both reserve and active, since the end of World War II.

Chapter 3

ORGANIZATION

U.S. Army soldiers from Company C, 2nd Battalion, 22nd Infantry Regiment, 1st BCT, 10th Mountain Division, and Iraqi Army (IA) soldiers look for training camps and weapon caches along the Zaghytun Chay River about fifty miles southeast of Kirkuk, Iraq. *Staff Sgt. Samuel Bendet*

10th Mountain Division (Light Infantry) "Climb to Glory"

The 10th Mountain Division (Light Infantry), based at Fort Drum, New York, is an infantry division that has been specifically designed to be rapidly deployable by strategic airlift to conduct a full range of operations from humanitarian relief to combat missions. Secretary of the Army Francis Harvey commented on the activities of the soldiers of the 10th Mountain Division: "Since the unit's reactivation in 1985, they have deployed for more real-world missions than any other division in the army. The 10th Mountain Division has gained a much-deserved reputation for rapid deployability, adaptable and flexible leaders and units, and the ability to accomplish the toughest missions."

Rapid deployment is the hallmark of the 10th Mountain Division. Within ninety-six hours of notification, the division is expected to deploy by air, sea, or land anywhere in the world. To meet these operational expectations, the division specifies elements that will deploy as the vanguard unit. At all times one of the 10th's infantry brigades is designated as the first infantry brigade to deploy (FIBTD), with one battalion task force within the brigade designated to be the first to deploy. The 10th Mountain Division is designated as a Force Package 3 unit and is considered a reinforcing combat unit or "follow-on force." The designation of Force Package 3 (FP 3) means the reinforcing force (RF) consists of the remaining continental U.S.-based (CONUS) divisions and those forces deployed forward in Europe. As the name implies, the RF is designed to provide a reinforcement capability to any theater of war.

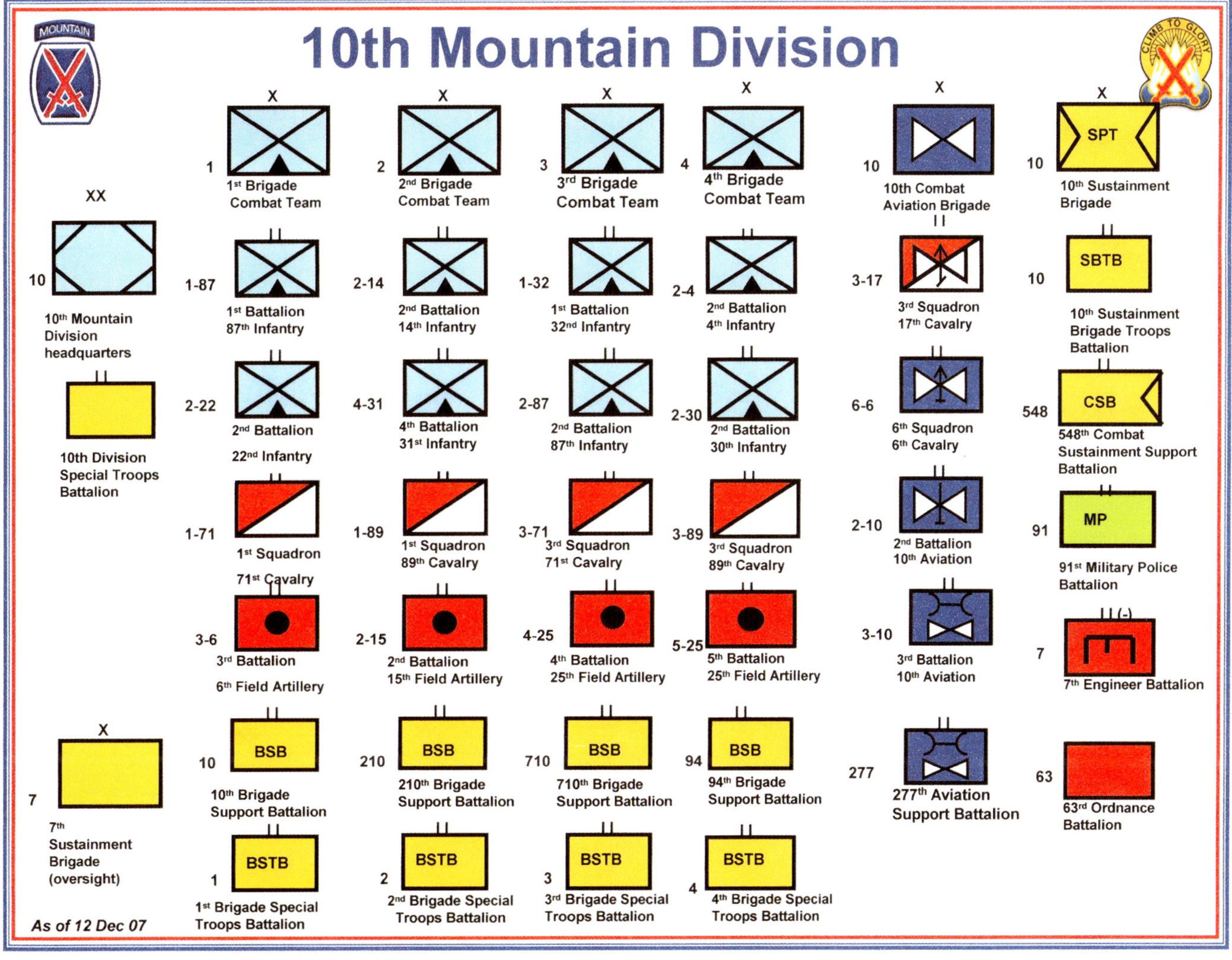

Specialist Daniel Parreira, 102nd Infantry Regiment, Connecticut National Guard, attached to Task Force Gauntlet, 10th Mountain Division, pulls security while Afghan National Police officers investigate a construction roadblock while on patrol in Bagram, Afghanistan. *Sgt. 1st Class Dexter D. Clouden*

This modular division concept is called the "brigade unit of action" and is part of an army-wide reorganization, changing brigade-sized elements into smaller, more modular forces that are then capable of deploying without the balance of the parent division.

The 10th Mountain Division officially transformed into the modular format on September 13, 2004. During this transformation, seven units were deactivated: Division Support Command; 3rd Battalion, 62nd Air Defense Artillery (ADA) Regiment; 110th Military Intelligence Battalion; 10th Signal Battalion; 41st Engineer Battalion; 10th Forward Support Battalion (FSB); and 710th Main Support Battalion. Additionally, thirteen units were activated: 3rd Brigade Combat Team (unit of action); 10th Mountain Division Support Brigade; Unit of Employment, Special Troops Battalion; 1st Squadron, 71st Cavalry Regiment; 10th Brigade Support Battalion; 1st Brigade Special Troops Battalion (BSTB); 2nd Squadron, 71st Cavalry Regiment; 2nd BSTB; 3rd Squadron, 71st Cavalry Regiment; 4th Battalion, 25th Field Artillery; 710th Brigade Support Battalion; 3rd BSTB; and the Support Brigade Special Troops Battalion.

10th Mountain Shoulder Patch

The shoulder insignia is a blue powder keg–shape design with a white border and two crossed bayonets. The blue background and the bayonets symbolize the infantry, while the position of the bayonets in a crossed position replicates the roman-numerical designation of the organization. The original insignia was approved for the 10th Light Division in January 1944. It was amended for the 10th Infantry Division in November 1984 and redesignated for the 10th Mountain Division in February 1985.

Worth noting is that the "mountain" tab used in the division shoulder patch is part of the division's heritage. According to Ben Able, 10th Mountain Division Public Affairs Office, "The tab is not to be confused with other tabs such as the Ranger, Airborne, or Special Forces tabs. The mountain tab is part of the patch for historical value and is not considered as a qualification."

One of the many faces of the 10th Mountain Division. Platoon leader First Lieutenant Ochman, from Company A, 2nd Platoon, 3rd Brigade Special Troops Battalion (BSTB), 10th Mountain Division, makes radio contact with his troops prior to beginning a search of local residences in the village of Stonaga, Afghanistan.
Spc. Christopher Barnhart

1st Brigade Combat Team—Warrior

The 1st Brigade Combat Team (BCT) was activated April 11, 1986, at Fort Drum, New York. The 1st Brigade is the command and control headquarters for Task Force Warrior. Its organic battalions consist of: 1/87th Infantry Battalion ("To the Top"), 2/22nd Infantry Battalion ("Deeds Not Words"), 1/71st Cavalry Squadron ("Ghost Squadron"), 3/6th Field Artillery Strike ("Swift and Bold"), 10th Brigade Support Battalion ("The Sherpa Battalion"), and 1st Brigade Special Troops Battalion ("Iroquois").

In January 2000, the brigade began its participation in the army's Joint Contingency Force advanced warfighting experiment. This ten-month period from January through October 2000 culminated in a Joint Readiness Center rotation where Task Force Warrior tested numerous "digital" concepts and items of equipment to help pave the way into the future for the light infantry.

2nd Brigade Combat Team

The mission of the 2nd Brigade Combat Team (BCT), 10th Mountain Division, is to conduct full spectrum counterinsurgency operations and defeat the anti-Iraqi government in order to allow the Iraqi government to assume primacy for independent security and governance.

A U.S. Army soldier prepares to enter a Taliban safehouse discovered during a patrol near the Pakistani border in the Paktika province of Afghanistan on March 30, 2007. The patrol is part of a mission intended to disrupt enemy movement in areas known to have enemy activity. The soldier is assigned to Company C, 2nd Battalion, 87th Infantry Regiment, 10th Mountain Division.
Staff Sgt. Justin Holley

An infantryman with the 4th Battalion, 31st Infantry Regiment ("Polar Bears"), 2nd BCT, 10th Mountain Division (Light Infantry), pulls security on the newly established battle position in Qarghulli, Iraq.
Staff Sgt. Angela McKinzie

The 2nd BCT was activated on October 7, 1985, at Fort Benning, Georgia, where it consisted of two battalions: the 2nd and 3rd battalions of the 14th Infantry. Later, a third battalion was added, the "Catamounts" of 2nd Battalion, 87th Infantry Regiment. In January 1989, the brigade relocated from Fort Benning to its current home at Fort Drum, New York.

In autumn 1989, the brigade deployed to Germany to participate in exercises Caravan Guard and Reforger. In 1990, the brigade participated in the 10th Mountain Division's first large-scale field-training exercise, Mountain Peak. During the Gulf War, the brigade sent 2nd Battalion, 14th Infantry Regiment, to the Multinational Force and Observer mission in the Sinai. In August 1991, the brigade deployed to Germany to participate in Reforger. In December 1991, 2nd Battalion, 14th Infantry Regiment, deployed to Guantanamo Bay, Cuba, in support of Haitian refugee operations. In August 1992, the brigade headquarters, 2nd Battalion, 14th Infantry Regiment, and 2nd Battalion, 87th Infantry Regiment, deployed to south Florida as a part of the Hurricane Andrew relief effort.

In December 1992, less than two months after returning from Florida, the brigade conducted a strategic deployment to Somalia in support of Operation Restore Hope. Operations Restore Hope and Continue Hope eventually saw all three battalions of the brigade engaged in combat operations. In July 1994, the brigade was alerted for contingency operations in the Republic of Haiti and began reorganization in preparation for their role in the advanced warfighting experiment. This culminated with the XVIII Airborne Corps emergency deployment readiness exercise "Dragon Team."

Since June 1997, 2nd Brigade has supported QRF missions in Bosnia and in the Sinai Peninsula with the Multinational Force and Observer mission. In 1998, the brigade deployed to a Joint Readiness Training Center rotation, executed the U.S. Military Academy support mission, and deployed to Operation Desert Fox in southwest Asia. The brigade deployed to Bosnia-Herzegovina from September 1999 to March 2000 in support of Operation Joint Endeavor, SFOR6. The 2nd BCT consists of: 2/14th Infantry Battalion ("Golden Dragons"), 4/31st Infantry Battalion ("Polar Bears"), 1/89th Cavalry RSTA (reconnaissance, surveillance, and target acquisition;

A U.S. Army soldier from Company B, 2nd Battalion, 87th Infantry Regiment, 3rd BCT, 10th Mountain Division, loads a mortar tube during combat operations to eliminate insurgents in the Paktika province of Afghanistan. *Spc. Ethan Anderson*

"Wolverines"), 2/15th Field Artillery Strike, 210th Brigade Support Battalion ("Commando Providers"), and the 2nd Brigade Special Troops Battalion.

3rd Brigade Combat Team ("Spartans")

The mission of the 3rd Brigade Combat Team (BCT) is to train and be ready for rapid deployment anywhere in the world to destroy the enemies of America in close combat. Units of the 3rd BCT are: 1/32nd Infantry Battalion ("Chosin"), 2/87th Infantry Battalion ("Catamounts"), 3/71st Cavalry RSTA ("Titans"), 4/25th Field Artillery Strike ("Wolfpack"), 710th Brigade Support Battalion ("Spartan Support"), and the 3rd Brigade Special Troops Battalion ("Vanguards").

4th Brigade Combat Team—Forged for War

The 4th Brigade Combat Team (BCT), 10th Mountain Division, also known as the Patriot Brigade, can rapidly deploy worldwide to conduct a full spectrum of operations

Two U.S. Army 2nd BCT, 10th Mountain Division, soldiers keep a sharp eye from their fighting position for other U.S. Army soldiers role-playing Iraqi insurgents during the simulated battle in Gahr Albai and Millawa Valley. These simulated battles take place on one of the ranges at the National Training Center (NTC), Fort Irwin, California, during Rotation 06-05, which is a training program conducted at the NTC to enhance a unit's desert war-fighting skills for future deployments. *Master Sgt. Johan Charles Van Boers*

to close with and destroy enemies of the United States. The BCT consists of: 2/4th Infantry Battalion ("Warriors"), 2/30th Infantry Battalion ("Wild Boars"), 3/89th Cavalry RSTA ("Sabers"), 5/25th Field Artillery Strike, 94th Brigade Support Battalion ("Strength"), and the 4th Brigade Special Troops Battalion ("Dagger").

Early in 2000, the U.S. Army began a program that redesigned the force structure of U.S. combat units. The army transformation initiatives were developed to create a highly mobile, more lethal, and more flexible capability that supported the rapid buildup of combat power wherever and whenever it was needed around the globe. Part of that transformation was the creation of new brigades called "units of action" in each of the ten army divisions. The 4th BCT is one of those new units. The structure of the brigade provides for organic infantry, cavalry, field-artillery, maintenance, logistic, and support capabilities.

On January 19, 2005, the 4th Brigade, 10th Mountain Division, was officially activated at Fort Polk, Louisiana. In the beginning they numbered a few hundred soldiers, with limited equipment, billeting, and physical office space for staff locations. With the United States fully committed to the Global War on Terrorism (GWOT), the brigade commanders immediately went to work rapidly building a combat power and capability that deploys at the direction of the commander in chief.

The 4th Brigade, along with its six subordinate battalions, conducted its first brigade-level exercise at Fort Chaffee, Arkansas, in April 2005. The levels of training and leadership in the brigade rose rapidly, and by the summer of 2005, soldiers conducted company-level, combined-arms live-fire exercises. During this time the brigade provided disaster response and relief in Louisiana in the aftermath of hurricanes Katrina and Rita in the fall of 2005. Soldiers deployed to New Orleans, as did the local Fort Polk community, to offer assistance. Once completed with the disaster relief mission, the soldiers returned to preparing for combat deployment at the second brigade-level exercise at the Joint Readiness Training Center in November 2005.

Since January 2006, the 4th BCT has deployed more than 2,500 soldiers in GWOT missions. Although the majority of theses soldiers have deployed to Afghanistan in support of Operation Enduring Freedom (OEF), many other soldiers of the 10th have also been sent to Iraq to assist in Operation Iraqi Freedom (OIF).

Private First Class Kevin Osborn, communications specialist, Headquarters and Headquarters Company, 2nd Battalion, 14th Infantry Regiment, 2nd BCT, 10th Mountain Division, Multi-National Division–Baghdad, makes adjustments to communications equipment at the Yusufiyah Power Plant. *Spc Rodney Foliente*

Throughout 2006, several formations within the 4th BCT carried out missions in Afghanistan. The brigade command and control headquarters established the first U.S. National Command Element in Kandahar in order to help transfer authority of combat operations to NATO-led coalition allies. The 94th Brigade Support Battalion conducted logistics support through convoy operations, aerial resupply, and forward-deployed support companies throughout thousands of square miles of southern and eastern Afghanistan.

During this time the 2/4th Infantry Battalion formed the nucleus of Task Force Warrior. This light infantry task force conducted combat and nation-building operations in Kabul and other provinces in southern Afghanistan as part of a multinational coalition brigade. Subsequently, Task Force Warrior moved to eastern Afghanistan to support operations being conducted by the 10th Mountain Division as part of Combined Joint Task Force 76. Task Force Warrior returned home in November 2006. Task Force Boar formed around 2/30th Infantry Battalion and then assumed authority from Task Force Warrior in eastern Afghanistan, where they conducted combat and nation-building operations to strengthen the growing Afghan government and civil authorities.

JRTC—Fort Polk

The Joint Readiness Training Center (JRTC) located at Fort Polk, Louisiana, focuses on improving unit readiness. This is accomplished through extremely realistic, stressful, and joint as well as combined training in combat arms. JRTC is one of the army's three "dirt" combat training centers resourced to train infantry brigade task forces and their subordinate elements in a joint, contemporary, operational environment. The other two locations are the National Training Center at Ft. Irwin, California, and the Combat Maneuver Training Center in Hohenfels, Germany.

Great emphasis is placed on realism as the JRTC provides rotational units (BlueFor) with the opportunity to conduct joint operations that emphasize contingency force missions. The training scenario is based on each of the participating organization's mission essential tasks list. Many of the exercises are mission rehearsals for actual operations the organization is scheduled to conduct.

The combat scenarios played out at JRTC allow the integration of air force and other military services as well as host-nation and civilian role players. The exercise scenarios duplicate many of the situations and challenges a unit may confront. Such scenarios may include host-national officials, citizens, insurgents and terrorists, news-media coverage, and nongovernmental organizations.

During the training, observer controllers (OCs) are responsible for keeping the scenarios realistic. These OCs will observe unit performance, control engagements and operations, teach doctrine, coach to improve unit performance, monitor safety, and conduct professional after action reviews (AARs). The OCs constantly strive for personal and professional development and are well-versed in current operational doctrine, tactics, techniques, and procedures.

The AARs provide immediate feedback for each element, from platoon through brigade task force. These reports provide impartial feedback that encourages interaction and discussion of unit strengths and weaknesses by all members of the unit. Every AAR focuses on a specific mission or system, identifying good and bad trends, and provides units the opportunity to determine not only what their weaknesses are but who is going to fix each weakness.

The OCs from the JRTC not only impart book smarts, they also bring back lessons learned from the mountain soldiers on the ground. Major Mike Kimball, an OC from JRTC, visited the commando area of operations under the 2nd Brigade Combat Team (BCT), 10th Mountain Division (Light Infantry) at Camp Striker, Iraq. To accomplish this task, a team of eight officers would spend twelve days down range in Iraq and Afghanistan areas of operation (AOs), discovering what works and what does not.

Major Kimball related, "We're here on a fact-finding mission. We strive to stay relevant because we're charged with training soldiers before they deploy. We're the busiest combat training center, and we must stay relevant. We send a smattering of people from different operations—information, aviation, fire support, and others. We converge on a chosen brigade and spread out to see how they're conducting operations. It's been absolutely invaluable. The team has spent time with plans officers, company commanders, and troops on the ground. Dismounted operations are key. No matter who you are, get out of the trucks, get out in the villages. Don't commute to work."

Lieutenant Colonel Dwight Duquesnay, the senior OC, commented, "Now we've seen it work. We can say, 'In country, they're doing this, and it works.' We were very well received by the units. The soldiers and leaders understand the importance of the training at the CTCs [counterterrorist centers] and bent over backward to integrate us. The brigade is performing very well. The brigade is in outstanding shape. Sometimes we come to a newly formed brigade, but this one is at its peak, operating at a very high level. It's refreshing to see. The lessons learned here are critical. It will allow us to improve the training at JRTC."

Commenting on the visit by the JRTC observers, Lt. Col. Daniel Goldthorpe, the 2nd BCT deputy commanding officer, stated, "Having the OCs visit was beneficial to the 2nd BCT as well. It was great to bounce ideas off them—another set of eyes, a different perspective. It allows us to put our combat experience back into the CTC so soldiers can learn from it."

Private First Class Ryan Mahan and Spc. Stephen McLain hoist Pfc. Ryan Springstead so he can look over a wall to see if they can enter a house through the roof of a building in Chinchal, Iraq. The soldiers are assigned to 3rd Platoon, Troop A, 1st Squadron, 71st Cavalry Regiment, 1st BCT, 10th Mountain Division.
Spc. Laura M. Buchta

Private First Class Christopher Edwards, a Sapper with Company A, 2nd BSTB, 2nd BCT, 10th Mountain Division (Light Infantry), rigs a bridge with explosives outside Quarghulli, Iraq. The 2nd BSTB soldiers air-assaulted into the village and worked with soldiers of Company D, 4th Battalion, 31st Infantry Regiment, 2nd BCT, to secure and destroy a bridge used by al-Qaeda to traffic foreign fighters and weapons into the southern belt of Baghdad. *Pvt. Jon Cano*

Soldiers and commanders of the 4th BCT served in Afghanistan to develop the relationships between coalition forces and the Afghan people. They conducted numerous humanitarian operations in distant and remote regions of the country. Soldiers in these operations provided medical and veterinary assistance; built schools and clinics; improved infrastructure such as roads, wells, and communication; and established trained and capable Afghan police, army, and civil leaders. In addition to reconstruction and humanitarian efforts, brigade soldiers conducted nonstop combat operations in order to improve the security situation and eliminate Taliban and al Qaeda networks and resistance.

10th Aviation Brigade

The brigade's mission is to maintain an aviation brigade trained and ready to deploy rapidly anywhere in the world to conduct combat. In addition, they provide combat support and combat service support for aviation operations to enable the 10th Mountain Division to fight and win. The 10th Aviation Brigade was activated at Griffis Air Force Base in Rome, New York, on July 2, 1988. It has played a key role in all the division's missions, as part of the SFOR6 in Bosnia-Herzegovina, Operation Restore Hope in Somalia, and Operation Uphold Democracy in Haiti. In each mission the brigade demonstrated the capability to rapidly deploy and conduct an aviation mission upon arrival in country.

The 10th Aviation Brigade is composed of the following units: Headquarters Company, 3rd Squadron 17th Cavalry Regiment ("Light Horse"), 6/6th Cavalry ("Six Shooters"), 2/10th Aviation Regiment ("Knighthawks"), 3/10th General Support Aviation Battalion ("Born of Fire"), and the 277th Aviation Support Battalion.

10th Sustainment Brigade ("Supporting the Climb")

The vision of the 10th Support Brigade is defined as: "We are warfighter logisticians and supporters prepared to give the shirts off our back and boots off our feet to support the fight. We will never say 'NO' as long as we have one gallon of gas to give or one bullet to give." The brigade includes Brigade Special Troops Battalion, 548th Combat Sustainment Support Battalion ("Supporting the Sword"), 10th Soldier Support Battalion ("Mountain Support"), and Military Police Battalion ("Mountain Guardians").

According to GlobalSecurity.org:

> The soldiers of the 10th Division Support Command (DISCOM), also known as the "Mule-

Private First Class Michael Fraser, infantryman, Company A, 2nd Battalion, 14th Infantry Regiment, 2nd BCT, 10th Mountain Division, Multi-National Division–Baghdad, looks through a scope as he watches his sector at the Yusufiyah Power Plant. *Spc Rodney Foliente*

skinners," trace their lineage to the Alpine infantrymen and their pack mules, which formed the Mountain Medical, Quartermaster, and Ordnance Maintenance Battalions that supported the 10th Infantry Division during World War II. The Division Trains, as they were called, were organized and assigned to the 10th Infantry Division on June 14, 1957, and were activated in Germany on July 1, 1957. Moving forward, they exchanged their stubborn mules for wheeled ambulances, trucks, and forklifts, and upon unit replacement in Germany, were deactivated at Fort Benning, Georgia, on June 14, 1958.

When the division was officially reactivated as the 10th Mountain Division in February 1985 at Fort Drum, New York, the Division Trains were redesignated as the 10th Division Support Command. The headquarters element organized with the 10th Supply and Transportation Battalion, the 10th Medical Battalion, and the 710th Maintenance Battalion, and then they became the 10th FSB, the 210th FSB, and the 710th Main Support Battalion, respectively. Divisional support was dedicated to the support of the mountain soldiers of this new light infantry division.

On August 16, 1987, the 548th Supply and Services Battalion was relocated from Fort McClellan, Georgia, to Fort Drum. In November 1993, the battalion was reorganized as the 548th Corps Support Battalion (CSB) and became part of the 10th DISCOM. Since its reactivation, the 10th DISCOM has secured a reputation of supporting the climb to glory. In September 1990, the 548th CSB deployed to southwest Asia for Operations Desert Shield and Desert Storm, providing critical combat service support to units operating in Saudi Arabia and Iraq. In 1992, elements of the 10th DISCOM were deployed to Florida in support of Hurricane Andrew relief operations. Equipped with a high level of expertise, they provided supply, maintenance, and medical support that rendered their services invaluable to the communities and lives they helped to rebuild. In December, the 10th DISCOM deployed again to Somalia in support of Operation Restore Hope.

The ranks and responsibilities of the Muleskinners grew dramatically as they sustained, maintained, and cared for several rotations of division soldiers while supporting humanitarian assistance to the local population.

In September 1994, the 10th DISCOM was called upon again and deployed with the division to Haiti in their traditional role as providers and sustainers, while also supporting humanitarian operations as part of Operation Uphold Democracy. In August 1999, elements of the 10th DISCOM deployed to the Balkans in support of peacekeeping operations as part of Task Force Eagle in Bosnia. In November 2001, elements from the 10th DISCOM deployed to Kosovo in support of Task Force Falcon.

Soldiers Creed/ Warriors Ethos

I am an American Soldier.

I am a Warrior and a member of a team. I serve the people of the United States and live the Army Values.

I will always place the mission first.

I will never accept defeat.

I will never quit.

I will never leave a fallen comrade.

I am disciplined, physically and mentally tough, trained, and proficient in my warrior tasks and drills. I always maintain my arms, my equipment, and myself.

I am an expert and I am a professional.

I stand ready to deploy, engage, and destroy the enemies of the United States of America in close combat.

I am a guardian of freedom and the American way of life.

I am an American Soldier.

Special Troops Battalion Deploy UAVs

Operating in Kirkuk, Iraq, soldiers from the 10th Mountain Division's 1st BCT, Special Troops Battalion, have become the commander's eyes on the battlefield, using the RQ-7 Shadow 200 tactical unmanned aerial vehicle (TUAV) to assist them in battling the insurgents. The Shadow has been instrumental in locating roadside improvised explosive devices (IEDs) and targets, as well as in tracking enemy movements and convoys.

The RQ-7 Shadow 200 is manufactured by AAI Textron. The Shadow 200 is eleven feet long with a wingspan of fourteen feet. Weighing 327 pounds, the compact TUAV can locate targets more than 125 kilometers away from the tactical operations center (TOC). The entire system consists of the TUAV, mission payloads of up to 50 pounds, ground control stations, launch/recovery equipment, and communication equipment. The system is highly mobile and can be transported in four M998 high-mobility multipurpose wheeled vehicles (HMMWVs, Humvees).

Operating the TUAVs from the safety of their patrol base, the soldiers view the video footage on television sets and computer monitors. The Shadow has a ceiling of fifteen thousand feet and can recognize vehicles up to eight thousand feet above ground level, both day and night. The use of such systems is a paradigm shift in the way the army conducts aerial reconnaissance, surveillance, target acquisition, and bomb-damage-assessment missions. The soldiers working in the ground-control stations can transmit near-real-time images and target data directly to orbiting joint surveillance target attack radar system (STAR) aircraft. On two occasions the battalion's unmanned aircraft system operators located enemy forces in the act of planting IEDs and then tracked their movement, which helped capture insurgents.

Army Sergeant First Class Nicholas Thornthwaite, the unmanned aircraft systems platoon sergeant in the

Sergeant First Class Nicholas Thornthwaite and Spc. William Arms, 1st BSTB, 10th Mountain Division, BSTB, and a civilian field representative for Aircraft Armaments Inc., prepare a Shadow 200 unmanned aircraft system for launch. The unit has used the Shadow to monitor the battlefield since its arrival in Iraq's Kirkuk province. *Spc Jason Jordan*

brigade's Special Troops Battalion, said, "The Shadow has been a tremendous asset to our brigade's combat operations. We have been able to get a picture of the battlefield before we send our troops outside the wire."

"We are similar to a TV crew, but with a much bigger mission. With these systems, we are able to stay on top, stay observant, and keep an eye out," said Sgt. Josh Nelson, UAS training, knowledge, and standardization operator.

UAS operator Spc. William Arms adds, "These systems give coalition forces the upper hand on the battlefield and save lives. When we discover an IED using the UAS, that is one less IED that can kill an American soldier. These systems give us a much-needed advantage. We are in the enemy's backyard, and we are unfamiliar with this terrain. Using the Shadow allows us to look around the corner without having to walk around out there. The guys on the ground still do the work; they have the tough job. We are here for them; we do our job for them. They are out there protecting us, and we are just trying to protect them, too."

Chapter 4

WEAPONS

U.S. Army Staff Sergeant Aldridge, of the 10th Mountain Division Special Troops Battalion, pulls security as Afghan National Army soldiers, U.S. Air Force airmen of the 755th Explosive Ordnance Disposal Unit, and U.S. Army soldiers of the 10th Mountain Division Special Troops Battalion move to an enemy weapons cache point on the side of a mountain in Mandikowl, Afghanistan. The soldier has the forward or vertical handgrip attached to the bottom of the RIS.
Staff Sgt. Marcus J. Quarterman

M9 Beretta

Since 1985, the M9 has seen service as the standard issue side arm for U.S. conventional and special troops in Operation Urgent Fury in Grenada, Operations Desert Shield and Desert Storm in Kuwait, Operation Restore Hope in Somalia, the Implementation Force (IFOR) in Bosnia, and the Kosovo Force (KFOR) in Kosovo. Currently, it is the issued side arm for Operations Enduring Freedom and Iraqi Freedom. Along with the standardization of the 9mm round, the M9 brought the armed forces a larger-capacity magazine. The M9 holds fifteen rounds compared to the Colt 1911's seven or eight rounds. Although the 9mm ammunition was lighter and smaller, it was viewed as adequate for line troops. This tradeoff also allowed the troops to engage more rounds in a firefight before needing to reload, with an average life of 72,250 rounds. The slide is open for nearly the entire length of the barrel. This facilitates the ejection of spent shells and virtually eliminates stoppages. The open slide configuration also provides a means for the pistol to be loaded manually.

Chief Warrant Officer Three Dean L. Leasure, Company A ("Rogues"), 1st Battalion, 10th Aviation Regiment, adjusts his individual body armor in preparation for a flight over the city of Mosul, Iraq. He is carrying an M9 Beretta 9mm semi-automatic pistol, which is the standard side arm of U.S. forces. *Capt. Scott M. Betts*

M16

The soldiers fighting with the 10th Mountain Division use both the M16 assault rifle and the M4 carbine. The unit the soldier is assigned to will determine which weapon will be used. Usually, the infantry will carry the M4, while support units carry the M16. The M16 is manufactured by either Colt Manufacturing or Fabrique Nationale. It has a length of thirty-nine inches and weighs less than nine pounds with a full thirty-round magazine. The maximum effective range of the weapon is eight hundred meters with a muzzle velocity of 853 meters per second. The M16A2 5.56mm rifle is a lightweight, air-cooled, gas-operated, magazine-fed, shoulder- or hip-fired weapon designed for either automatic fire (three-round bursts) or semiautomatic fire (single shot). The weapon has a fully adjustable rear sight. The bottom of the trigger guard opens to provide access to the trigger while wearing winter mittens. The upper receiver/barrel assembly has a fully adjustable rear sight and a compensator, which helps keep the muzzle down during firing. The steel bolt group and barrel extension are designed with locking lugs that lock the bolt group to the barrel extension, allowing the rifle to have a lightweight aluminum receiver.

M4

The lineage of the M4 goes back almost five decades to the mid-fifties when the U.S. military sought a weapon to replace the heavy M14 battle rifle; in 1959, that weapon, the M16 rifle was born. A product of Eugene Stoner, this lightweight assault weapon was viewed with apprehension when first introduced. Soldiers used to the heavy M1 and M14 rifles often referred to it as a "toy gun," As the war continued, other modifications of the M16 series were developed, and the XM177E1 was introduced to the U.S. troops. This shortened version of the M16 with a collapsible stock and various barrel lengths was often referred to as the Colt automatic rifle-15 (CAR-15). The CAR-15 saw service with the SEALs (sea-air-land teams), long range reconnaissance patrols (LRRP), study and observation groups (SOG), and other special operations soldiers. This carbine version of the M16 laid the groundwork for the Colt M4 carbine in use today, which has evolved into the weapon of choice for today's special operations forces in general as well as the for airborne infantry.

The primary rifle used by the 10th Mountain Division is the Colt M4 carbine. This shortened version of the M16A2 rifle features a collapsible stock, a flat top upper receiver with an accessory rail, and a detachable handle/rear aperture sight assembly. Private First Class Andrew Kring, a military police soldier with the 1/10th Mountain Division's BSTB, is armed with a stock M4. He scans his sector as he conducts dismounted security on election day in the Abu Ghraib area of western Baghdad. *Spc. Emily Wilsoncroft*

Using the RIS, numerous accessories can be added to the weapon. This M4 carbine is equipped with advanced combat optical gunsight (ACOG), PAQ-2 infrared aiming device, and vertical foregrip. Sergeant First Class Ralph Roe, a Headquarters and Headquarters Company, 4th Battalion, 31st Infantry Regiment, 2nd BCT, 10th Mountain Division scout platoon sergeant and native of Bloomingburg, New York, pulled security from a boat as he traveled down the Euphrates River in Iraq. *Staff Sgt. Angela McKinzie*

Soldiers of the 10th Mountain Division are currently issued the M4 carbine. The M4 from Colt Arms of Connecticut is a smaller, more compact version of the full-sized M16A2 rifle. This weapon was design specifically for the U.S Special Operations Forces (SOF); however because of its introduction, the weapon has found its way into conventional units. The carbine is designed for when speed of action and light weights are required. The difference between the M4 and the M4A1, which is the primary weapon for U.S. SOF units, is that vthe M4 fire selector is safe-semi-burst, while the M4A1 is safe-semi-auto. A 10th Mountain veteran commented, "We did not use the M4 that is fully automatic and to me that is a waste of ammunition. We could fire on burst if need be, but usually we just fired on semi-automatic; this was more accurate and jams the weapon less. Not to mention it saves ammo."

The barrel has been redesigned to a shortened 14.5 inches, which reduces the weight while maintaining its effectiveness for quick handling during field operations. The retractable butt stock has intermediate stops allowing versatility in military operations on urban terrain (MOUT) without compromising shooting capabilities.

The M4 has a rifling twist of one in seven inches, making it compatible with the full range of 5.56mm ammunitions. Its sighting system contains dual apertures, allowing for zero to two hundred meters and a smaller opening for engaging targets at a longer range of five hundred to six hundred meters.

Special Operations Peculiar Modification (SOPMOD) Accessory Kit

Regarding the SOPMOD kit, Chris McGurk, a combat veteran with the 10th, related, "Some of us referred to the kits that way, but a majority of the guys just called the items by their names," that is, ACOG, M68 Aimpoint, and so forth.

The SOPMOD accessory kit allows the soldier to modify the weapon per mission parameters. Using the rail interface system (RIS), numerous components of the kit may be secured to the weapon. The kit includes a 4x32mm Trijicon day optical scope, allowing the soldiers to judge range and deliver more accurate fire out to three hundred meters; Trijicon reflex sight, designed for close-in engagement; and an infrared target pointer/illuminator/aiming laser AN/PEQ-2 (for use with night vision devices), which places a red aiming dot on the target, and is therefore very useful in MOUT environments. Additionally, it is equipped with visible light, a high-intensity flashlight mounted on the rail system; backup iron sight—because the carrying handle of the M4 can be removed, this backup sight can be employed

Trijicon ACOG's 4x32 scope provides increased hit potential in all lighting conditions. This reticle provides increased capability to direct, identify, and hit targets to the maximum effective range of the M4 carbine (six hundred meters). Specialist Scott with Battery A, 2nd Battalion, 15th Artillery Regiment, 2nd BCT, 10th Mountain Division, checks down range using his scope during a combined mission with the IA near Yusufiyah, Iraq. *Sgt. Martin Newton*

in the absence of the handle; and a forward hand grip, which helps to stabilize the weapon and keeps the user's hands away from the hand guards and barrel, which tends to heat up in combat.

The M4 carbine is a most capable and deadly weapon suitable to infantry missions. The U.S. Army Special Operations Command (USASOC) wanted to make the weapon even more effective for both close-in engagements and long-range targets. To accomplish this, the U.S. Special Operations Command (USSOCOM) and the Crane Division, Naval Surface Warfare Center, developed the SOPMOD accessory kit. Introduced in 1994, the SOPMOD kit is issued to all U.S. SOF to expand on the capabilities and operation of the M4 carbine.

The SOPMOD kit consists of numerous components that may be attached directly on the M4 carbine or attached to the RIS. These various accessories give the shooter the flexibility to choose the appropriate optics, lasers, lights, and so forth, depending on mission parameters. The SOPMOD kit is constantly being evaluated, and research is ongoing to further enhance the operability, functionality, and lethality of the M4 carbine.

Rail Interface System (RIS)

The rail interface system (RIS) is a notched rail system that replaces the front hand guards on the M4 receiver. This rail system is located on the top, bottom, and sides of the barrel; it helps attach the SOPMOD kit components on

The Comp-M sight superimposes a red dot on the target, allowing the soldier to adjust his weapon when required in the fast-pace shooting environment of military operations urban terrain (MOUT). The weapon is also equipped with an M203 40mm grenade launcher. Private Barnhill of Battery A, 2nd Battalion, 15th Artillery Regiment, 2nd BCT, 10th Mountain Division, scans ahead in the prone position during a combined mission with the IA in Yusufiyah, Iraq. *Sgt. Martin Newton*

any of the four sides. The notches are numbered, making it possible to attach and reattach the various components at the same position each time it is mounted. Optical sights and night vision devices can be mounted on the top, while top and side rails would be the choice for positioning laser aiming devices or lights. The bottom of the RIS normally will accommodate the vertical grip or lights. When no accessories are mounted to the RIS, plastic hand guards are emplaced to provide cover and protect the unused portions of the rail. A newer version of the RIS is the rail adapter system (RAS). The primary difference between the two is that the RAS is mounted to the weapon and the numbering setup.

ACOG (Advance Combat Optical Gunsight)

The ACOG, manufactured by Trijicon, is the day optical scope for the SOPMOD accessory kit. The ACOG is a four-power telescopic sight, which includes a ballistic compensating reticle. Using this reticle provides increased capability to direct, identify, and hit targets up to six hundred meters, the maximum effective range of the M4 carbine. As a backup, the ACOG is equipped with an iron sight for rapid close range engagement (CRE). Both the front iron sight and the scope reticle provide target recognition and standoff attack advantage while retaining a close-quarters capability equivalent to the standard iron sights.

Specialist Jason Curtis from the 10th Mountain Division pulls security for fellow soldiers patroling Parun, Afghanistan. He is armed with an M249 squad automatic weapon (SAW) and an M9 Berretta pistol. On top of the SAW is mounted an EOTech holographic display sight. The heads-up display allows the soldier to acquire the target faster than with traditional iron sights. *Sgt. Brandon Aird*

M68 Aimpoint COMP-M

The Aimpoint Comp-M is in use for MOUT activities. After extensive testing, the U.S. Army adopted the Aimpoint Comp-M as its red dot sighting system. Using an eyes-open-and-head-up method, the shooter is able to acquire the target with excellent speed and accuracy. The Comp-M sight superimposes a red dot on the target that the brain sees, allowing the soldier to adjust his weapon accordingly when required in the fast-pace shooting environment of close-quarters combat. The Comp-M is parallax free, which means the shooter does not have to compensate for parallax deviation. The sight may be mounted on the carrying handle or RIS of the rifle.

Holographic Display Sight (HDS)

Manufactured by EOTech, the holographic display sight (HDS), as the name implies, displays holographic patterns, which have been designed for instant target acquisition under any lighting situations, without covering or obscuring the point of aim. The holographic reticle can be seen through the sight, providing the soldier with a large view of the target or zone of engagement. Unlike other optics, the HDS is passive and emits no telltale signature. The heads-up, rectangular, full view of the HDS eliminates any blind spots, constricted vision, or tunnel vision normally associated with cylindrical sights. Chris McGurk, a combat veteran with the 10th, said, "The holographic site I used was a better quality and

The AN/PEQ-2 infrared target pointer/illuminator/aiming laser (ITPIAL) allows the M4 to be effectively employed to three hundred meters with standard issue night vision goggles (NVG) or a weapon-mounted night vision device, that is, an AN/PVS-14. The AN/PEQ-2, or "Pac2" as it is called, can be used as a pointing device to signal to helicopters, gun ships, and jets during close air support. Army Staff Sergeant Sean Lepper, a squad leader with 1st Platoon, Company C, 2nd Battalion, 87th Infantry Regiment, 3rd BCT, 10th Mountain Division, pulls security during a stop. *Spc. Matthew Leary*

I could use it much better with both eyes open, not to mention I preferred the night-vision capability. Using both eyes open, the soldier can sight in on the target for a true two-eye operation."

The wide field of view of the HDS allows the shooter to sight-in on the target and the target area while maintaining peripheral viewing through the sight if needed, up to 350 degrees off axis. A unique feature of the HDS is the fact that it works if the heads-up display window is obstructed by mud, snow, and so forth. Even if the laminated window is shattered, the sight remains fully operational, with the point of aim being maintained. It can be used in conjunction with night vision goggles/night vision device (NVG/NVD). The hallmarks of the HDS are speed and ease of use equating incredible accuracy and instant sight-on target operation, which can be the difference between life and death in MOUT operations.

Visible Light Illuminator (VLI)

The visible light illuminator (VLI) provides white light to help soldiers move inside dark buildings, bunkers, and tunnels. It is useful for searching and identifying targets. It has a dual-battery capability, meaning it can be power by three 3-volt lithium DL123 batteries or six 1.5-volt AA batteries. The VLI is most useful in military operations other than war, or in low-intensity conflicts, when search and clear operations may be complicated by tripwires, booby traps, and noncombatants, and the danger of revealing your position is offset by the need for better vision than is possible with night vision goggles. The intense white light can overwhelm an opponent in MOUT, giving the soldier a momentary advantage. An infrared (IR) filter can be attached to provide short-range illumination (fifty meters) when using night vision equipment. This red filter also reduces glare in smoky environments and reduces impact on the shooter's night vision.

AN/PEQ-2 Infrared Illuminator/ Aiming Laser

The AN/PEQ-2 infrared target pointer/illuminator/ aiming laser (ITPIAL) allows the M4 to be effectively employed to three hundred meters with standard issue NVG or a weapon-mounted night vision device, such as an AN/PVS-14. The IR illuminator broadens the capabilities

First Sergeant Jamie Nakano, Company B, 1st Battalion, 32nd Infantry Regiment, 10th Mountain Division, and an Afghan interpreter negotiate the mountainous terrain of the Nuristan province while on patrol in Aranas, Afghanistan. Note he has installed a bipod on the RIS of his M4. *Spc. Eric Jungels*

of the NVGs in buildings, tunnels, jungle, overcast, and other low-light conditions where starlight would not be sufficient to support night vision, and it allows visibility in areas normally in shadow. At close range, a neutral-density filter is used to eliminate glare around the aiming laser to improve the view of the target for identification, as well as for precision aiming. This combination provides the soldier a decisive advantage over an opposing force with little or no night-vision capability.

Visible Laser AN/PEQ-5

The AN/PEQ-5, as the name implies, is a visible laser that attaches to the RIS and provides a close-range visible laser-aiming beam. The VL can be used at close range in a lighted building, in darkness with the visible light illuminator, or at night with night vision equipment. It is used primarily in MOUT, where it provides a fast and accurate means of aiming the weapon. It is especially valuable when the soldier is wearing a protective mask, firing from an awkward position, or firing from behind cover and around corners. It permits the shooter to focus all his attention on the target while being able to accurately direct the point of impact. Because it is visible, it does provide a nonlethal show of force that can intimidate hostile personnel, that is, letting the "bad guys" know you have them in your sights.

Forward Handgrip

The forward or vertical handgrip attaches to the bottom of the RIS and provides added support, giving the shooter a more stable firing platform. It can be used as a monopod

Specialist Justin McElroy (left), a team leader from Fayetteville, Tennessee; soldiers from 3rd Platoon, Combat Company, 1st Battalion, 32nd Infantry; and Afghan National Army troops negotiate the tough Afghan terrain during a patrol near the village of Tsapre in eastern Afghanistan. The patrol was part of a mission that included air assaults and patrols in remote villages throughout the region and allowed coalition forces to engage the local population. *Spc. Jon Arguello*

Sergeant Angel Maldonado assists Lt. Col. Michael Price in climbing a cliff to the weapons cache. Note the lieutenant colonel is armed with a commando version of the M4. This weapon has the shorter ten-inch barrel, compact and good for close-in fighting. *Staff Sgt. Marcus J. Quarterman*

in a supported position and allows the soldier to hold the weapon despite overheating. The forward handgrip can be used to push against the assault sling and stabilize the weapon with isometric tension during MOUT. With numerous modifications available, it does tend to make the soldier want to use them all; it is not uncommon to see a soldier with as many of the SOPMOD accessories on the M4 as he can fit. One of the negatives of the vertical grip is the possibility of it catching on a ledge or the edge of the helicopter during entry or extraction.

Backup Iron Sight (BUIS)

The backup iron sight (BUIS) supplies aiming ability similar to the standard iron sight on the carbine to three hundred meters. The BUIS folds out of the way to allow the day optical scope or reflex sight and night vision devices to be mounted on the M4 carbine. If the optical scopes are damaged or otherwise rendered inoperable, they can be removed and the BUIS will then be used to complete the mission. The sight can also be used to bore sight or confirm zero on the reflex sight or visible laser.

AN/PVS-14 Night Vision Device (NVD)

The AN/PVS-14 is the optimum night vision monocular ensemble for special applications. The monocular or pocket-scope can be handheld, head-mounted, helmet-mounted, or attached to a weapon. The new PVS-14D NVD offers the latest, state-of-the-art capability in a package that meets the rigorous demands of the mountain soldiers. The monocular configuration is important to shooters who want to operate with night vision while maintaining dark adaptation in the opposite eye. The head-mount assembly, a standard in the kit, facilitates hands-free operation when helmet wear is not required. The weapon mount allows for use in a

The AN/PVS-14 is the optimum night vision monocular ensemble for special applications. The monocular or pocket-scope can be handheld, facemask-mounted, helmet-mounted, or attached to a weapon. *Petty Officer 1st Class Michael B. W. Watkins*

The M14 rifle was the standard service rifle until it was replaced in the late 1960s by the M16A1 rifle. Private Samuel Glanzer conducts security while the pick-up zone is established along the Zaghytun Chay River, about fifty miles southeast of Kirkuk, Iraq, on November 20, 2007. Glanzer is a designated marksman from Company C, 2nd Battalion, 22nd Infantry Regiment, 1st BCT, 10th Mountain Division. *Staff Sgt. Samuel Bendet*

variety of applications, from using your iron sights to coupling with a red dot or tritium sighting systems, such as the Aimpoint Comp M/M, Trijicon ACOG system, and EOTech HDS. A compass is available to allow the user to view the bearing in the night vision image.

M203 Grenade Launcher

The M203 grenade launcher is a lightweight (three pounds), single-shot, breech-loaded 40mm weapon specifically designed for placement beneath the barrel of the M16A1 and M16A2 rifles and M4/M16A2 carbines. With a quick-release mechanism, the addition of the M203 to the M16 rifle or M4 carbine creates the versatility of a weapon system capable of firing 5.56mm ammunition, as well as an expansive range of 40mm high-explosive (HE) and special-purpose munitions.

The most commonly used ammunition is the M406 antipersonnel round. This grenade has a deadly radius of five meters. In addition to its fragmentation effects, the M433 multipurpose grenade is capable of penetrating a steel-armor plate up to two inches thick. Other types of ordnance available are buckshot, tear gas, and various signal rounds.

A soldier from Company C, 4th Battalion, 31st Infantry Regiment, 2nd BCT, 10th Mountain Division, prepares to perform a foot patrol in Yusufiyah, Iraq. He is armed with a modified M14 in a Sage Industries stock. The updated stock provides the sniper with a Picitinny rail system for the mounting of optics, laser-aiming devices, and other accessories. *Sgt. Tierney Nowland*

The receiver of the M203 is manufactured of high-strength forged aluminum alloy. This provides extreme ruggedness while keeping weight to a minimum. A complete self-cocking firing mechanism, including striker, trigger, and positive safety lever, is included in the receiver. This will allow the M203 to be operated as an independent weapon, even though attached to the M16A1/M16A2 rifles and M4/M16A2 carbines. The barrel is also made of high-strength aluminum alloy, which has been shortened from twelve to nine inches, allowing for improved balance and handling. It slides forward in the receiver to accept a round of ammunition and then slides backward to automatically lock in the closed position, ready to fire.

The quick attach/detach M203 mount and leaf sight, when combined with the standard M203 grenade launcher, provides additional firepower to the soldier, giving him both a point and area engagement capability. The most commonly used ammunition is the high-explosive, dual-purpose (HEDP) M406 40mm projectile. This grenade has a deadly radius of five meters and is used as antipersonnel and anti-light armor. Additional projectiles include M381 HE; M386 HE; M397 airburst; M397A1 airburst; M433 HEDP; M441 HE; M576 buckshot; M583A1 40mm star parachute round for illumination; M651 CS; M661 green star cluster; M662 red star cluster; M676 yellow smoke canopy; M680 white smoke canopy; M682 red smoke canopy; M713 red ground marker; M715 green ground marker; M716 yellow ground marker; M781 practice; M918 target practice; M992 infrared illuminant cartridge (IRIC); 40mm nonlethal round; 40mm canister round; and 40mm sponge grenade.

M249 SAW is an individually portable, air-cooled, belt-fed, gas-operated light machine gun that fires from the open-bolt position. The standard ammunition load is two hundred rounds of 5.56mm ammunition in disintegrating belts, alternating four round full metal jacket and one round tracer. Specialist Joby Jose of A Battery, 2nd Battalion, 15th Artillery Regiment, 2nd BCT, 10th Mountain Division, focuses down range during a combined mission with the IA in Lutafiyah, Iraq. *Sgt. Martin Newton*

This grenade has a deadly radius of three meters. Future development in 40mm grenades will introduce airburst capability, which will provide increased lethality and bursting radius through prefragmented, programmable HE warheads.

The quick attach M203 combines flexibility and deadliness to the individual weapon. Using multiple M203 setups allows concentrated fire by bursting munitions, which are extremely useful in raids and ambushes, and provides the ability to illuminate or obscure the target while simultaneously delivering continuous HEDP fire. The M203 grenade leaf sight attaches to the RIS for fire control.

M14

The M14 dates back to 1957, when the U.S. Army selected it as the standard service rifle for the infantry. It was to be a replacement for the M1 Garand and M1918 Browning automatic rifle (BAR). General George S. Patton said, "The M1 rifle is the greatest battle implement ever devised." It could be argued that the general might have had a similar view of the M14 had he been around to witness its evolution. The M14 was the main battle rifle until the late 1960s, when it was replaced by the M16 assault rifle during the Vietnam War. While the majority of the soldiers and Marines in-country were issued the "black rifle," the M14 continued to be used on a limited basis by small amounts of elite teams throughout the war.

After the war in southeast Asia, the M14 rifles were relegated into the background, often surfacing to appear at shooting competitions. The M16 and newer CAR-15 versions had all but replaced the heavy wooden-stocked

The M240B, by Fabrique Nationale, has replaced the aging M60 machine gun. This 7.62mm machine gun delivers more energy to the target than the smaller-caliber M249 SAW. Private First Class Justin Hall (left) and Spc. Austin Clapp, members of 3rd Platoon, Combat Company, 1st Battalion, 32nd Infantry, man a M240B fighting position while the platoon leader holds talks with the village elders. *Spc. Jon Arguello*

weapon, but the M14 found a home with the SOF. It was not uncommon to find the heavy hitting weapon among SEAL teams and Ranger platoons. The weapon eventually found a home in conventional infantry units as well.

The M14 rifle is a gas-operated shoulder-fired weapon, firing a 7.62mm round from a twenty-round magazine. The rifle is capable of semiautomatic and full-automatic fire via a selector on the right side of the weapon. The rifle weighs in at eleven pounds with full magazine and sling. It has a cyclic rate of fire of 750 rounds per minute with an effective range of four hundred meters. Variations to the standard M14 can be seen in the designated marksman rifle, as well as the M21 and enhanced battle rifle.

M21

The M21 is a product of the Vietnam War, developed jointly by the Army Weapons Command, Rock Island, Illinois; Combat Development Command, Ft. Benning, Georgia; and the Limited Warfare Agency, Aberdeen, Maryland. During the Vietnam War, it was the primary sniper rifle of the U.S. Army and remained such until replaced by the M24 sniper weapon system (SWS) in 1988. The M21 remains in service with the 10th Mountain Division as well as other elite units and some SOF units. The M21 7.62mm SWS consists of a national match M14 and scope. The M21 is accurized by the U.S. Army Marksmanship Training Unit and shares the basic specifications and operations of the standard M14. The M21 is significantly different from the M14. The

U.S. Army Sergeant Gerado Alvarado, 2nd Battalion, 15th Field Artillery Regiment, 2nd BCT, 10th Mountain Division out of Fort Drum, New York, provides security with his .50-caliber rifle during a medical civic action program in Mahmudiyah, Iraq. *Master Sgt. Jonathan Doti*

M21's barrel is selected and gauged to ensure specific tolerances and is also not chromium-plated. The stock of the weapon is filled with epoxy, and the receiver is individually fitted to the walnut stock with a fiberglass compound. The gas cylinder and piston are modified and polished to reduce carbon buildup and improve the operation of the weapon.

Enhanced Battle Rifle (EBR)

This modified M14 was a result of the small arms section of the U.S. Navy Cranes Surface Warfare Center's effort to give a new lease on life to the M14 assault rifle. Crane teamed up with Sage International, Ltd. to create the EBR. Originally designed by Crane for the SEAL and Marine Force Recon community, the EBR has found its way into many of the conventional units. The EBR uses a unique Sage stock, which allows the barrel, receiver, and trigger group to be installed. The stock features four Mil-Standard 1913 Picatinny rails, which surround the barrel, and an additional rail above the receiver to accommodate the placement of night-vision devices and other optics. The Sage stock incorporates a pistol grip and retractable stock, which facilitates the length of pull (LOP) and a check weld for the shooter.

The EBR (without scope or added devices) weighs in at less than twelve pounds, with a twenty-two-inch, regular M14 barrel. The addition of the Sage stock provides the shooter with a straight line over the previous wooden stock, reducing the felt recoil of the 7.62mm round.

M24 Sniper Weapon System (SWS)

The current issue sniper rifle for the army is the M24 sniper weapon system (SWS). The M24 is based on the Remington 700 series long action. This action accommodates chambering for either the 7.62x51mm or .300 Winchester Magnum round. The rifle is a bolt-action six-shot repeating rifle (one round in the chamber and five additional rounds in the magazine). It is issued with the Leupold Mark IV 10-power M3A scope, commonly referred to as the "Ma-3-Alpha." Additionally, the sniper may make use of the metallic iron sights. Attached to the scope is the M24/EMA ARD

The M136 AT4 is a lightweight, self-contained, man-portable, antiarmor weapon. Inside of the expendable, one-piece fiberglass-wrapped tube is a free-flight, fin-stabilized, rocket-type cartridge. The launcher is watertight for ease of transportation and storage. Unlike the M72-series light antitank weapon (LAW), the AT4 launcher does not need to be extended before firing. With a range of 2,100 meters, the warhead is capable of penetrating 400mm of rolled homogenous armor. *Author's collection*

(anti-reflection device), less than three inches long, this honeycomb of tubes cuts down the glare of the scope. The M24 SWS comes with a Harris bipod; however, most of the time, the bipod remains in the deployment case. The rifle weighs 12.1 pounds without the scope and has an overall length of forty-three inches, with a free-floating barrel of twenty-four inches. The stock is a composite of Kevlar, graphite, and fiberglass with an aluminum bedding block. The stock has an adjustable butt plate to accommodate the LOP.

M110 Semiautomatic Sniper System (SASS)

The soldiers have begun to field a new sniper rifle, the M110 semiautomatic sniper system (SASS). The rifle itself is manufactured by Knight's Armament Company (KAC) in Titusville, Florida. The complete system includes Leupold daytime optics, Harris swivel bipods, AN/PVS-14 (Army-Navy passive viewing system) night sights, as well as other SOPMOD accessories. The rifle has ambidextrous features, such as a double-sided magazine release and safety selector switch.

Based on the design of the original AR-10 by Eugene Stoner, the M110 is much more than an M16 on steroids. The rifle is similar to Knight's SR-25 and Mk 11 Mod 0 semiautomatic precision rifles, but differs significantly in butt stock and rail system design. The M110 features additional refinements designed by KAC to maximize parts commonality with the AR15/M16, improve weapon reliability, and increase accuracy.

According to GlobalSecurity.org, the M110 SASS's features include a rapid fire/rapid reload, suppressed sniper rifle; a greater rate of fire and lethality than that of the M24 SWS; reduced weight, primarily antipersonnel at ranges equal to or greater than the M24; an enhanced sniper-spotting scope system; a folding detachable bipod; five-, ten-, and twenty-round capacity detachable magazines; barrel life greater than five thousand rounds; variable-power day optic scope; detachable weapon suppressor; and integrated Mil-STD 1913 rail system, all packaged in a hard case for storage and transportation.

M249 Squad Automatic Weapon (SAW)

Fielded in the mid-1980s, the M249 SAW is an individually portable, air-cooled, belt-fed, gas-operated light machine gun. A unique feature of the SAW is the number of alternate ammunition feeds. The standard ammunition load is two hundred rounds of 5.56mm ammunitions in disintegrating belts. These rounds are fed from a two-hundred-round plastic ammunition box and through the side of the weapon. The normal link ammunition for the SAW is four rounds of M855 ball ammunitions, followed by one round of M85 tracer. Additionally, it can use standard twenty- and thirty-round M16 magazines, which are inserted in a magazine well in the bottom of the SAW. Utilizing the same 5.56mm ammunition as the M4, it allows the platoon to carry common ammunition loads. The M249 is capable of engaging targets out to eight hundred meters.

M240 Medium Machine Gun

After extensive operational testing, the U.S. Army selected the M240B medium machine gun as a replacement for the M60 family of machine guns. Manufactured by Fabrique Nationale, the 24.2-pound M240B medium machine gun is a gas-operated, air-cooled, linked belt-fed weapon that fires the 7.62x51mm round. The weapon fires from an open-bolt position with a maximum effective range of 1,100 meters. The rate of fire is adjustable from 750 to 1,400 rounds per minute through an adjustable gas regulator. It features a folding bipod that attaches to the receiver; a quick-change barrel assembly; a feed cover and bolt assembly, enabling closure of the cover regardless of bolt position; a plastic butt stock; and an integral optical sight rail. Although it possesses many of the same characteristics as the older M60, the durability of the M240 system results in superior reliability and maintainability.

AT4

The M136 AT4 is the army's principal light antitank weapon, providing precision delivery of an 84mm HE antiarmor warhead with negligible recoil. The M136 AT4 is a man-portable, self-contained, antiarmor weapon consisting of a free flight, fin-stabilized, rocket-type cartridge packed in an expendable, one-piece, fiberglass-wrapped tube. Unlike the M72 LAW (light antitank weapon), the AT4 launcher does not need to be extended before firing. When the warhead makes impact with the target, the nosecone crushes and the impact sensor will activate the internal fuse. Upon ignition, the piezoelectric-fuse element triggers the detonator initiating the main charge. This results in penetration where the main charge fires. The warhead body propels into a directional gas jet that is capable of penetrating more than seventeen inches of armor plate; this results in "spalling," the projecting incendiary fragments generate blinding light and obliterate the interior of the target.

Javelin

The Javelin is a man-portable, highly lethal, and survivable medium antitank weapon system used by the infantry, scouts, and combat engineers. The system entered army service in 1996. The Javelin is the first "fire-and-forget" shoulder-fired antitank missile now fielded by the U.S. Army and U.S. Marine Corps, replacing Dragon. Javelin's unique top-attack flight mode, superior self-guiding tracking system, and advanced warhead design allow it to defeat all known tanks out to ranges of 2,500 meters.

The two major components of the Javelin are a reusable command launch unit (CLU) and a missile sealed in a disposable launch tube assembly. The CLU's integrated day/night sight provides target engagement capability in adverse weather and countermeasure environments. The CLU also may be used by itself for battlefield surveillance and reconnaissance.

The Javelin is fielded with no specific test measurement or diagnostic equipment—allowing our forces to deploy rapidly and unencumbered. Javelin's fire-and-forget guidance mode enables gunners to fire and then immediately take cover, greatly increasing survivability. Special features include a selectable top-attack or direct-fire mode (for targets under cover or for use in urban terrain against bunkers and buildings), target lock-on before launch, and a very limited back blast that enables gunners to safely fire from enclosures and covered fighting positions. Javelins can also be installed on tracked, wheeled, or amphibious vehicles. It requires a crew of two to operate. Including the missile and CLU, a javelin weighs 49.5 pounds, is 3 feet 6 inches long, and has a range in excess of 2,500 meters.

The Javelin is the first "fire-and-forget" shoulder-fired anti-tank missile now fielded to the U.S. Army and U.S. Marine Corps, replacing Dragon. Javelin's unique top-attack flight mode, superior self-guiding tracking system, and advanced warhead design allows it to defeat all known tanks out to ranges of 2,500 meters. *U.S. Army photo*

M18A1 "Claymore" Mine

The M18A1 mine, more commonly referred to as the Claymore mine, is primarily employed as a defensive weapon. It has, however, been known to be employed in certain situations as an offensive weapon. The M18A1 can be deployed as a mine, an offensive weapon, or a booby trap; it also has use as a pursuit deterrence device. Additionally, the Claymore can be command detonated and has the capability of being sighted directionally to provide fragmentation over a specific target area.

The M18A1 antipersonnel mine is a curved, rectangular, plastic case that contains a layer of composition C3 explosive; packed in the explosive are seven hundred steel balls. The front face containing the steel balls is designed to produce an arc-shaped spray, which can be aimed at a predetermined target area. It comes in a bandoleer, which includes the M18A1 mine, an M57 firing device, an M40 test set, and an electrical blasting cap assembly.

60mm Mortar

The M224 60mm lightweight mortar is a smooth-bore, muzzle-loading, high-angle-of-fire weapon. Its purpose is to provide the company commander with an indirect-fire weapon. The cannon assembly is composed of the barrel, combination base cap, and firing mechanism. The mount consists of a bipod and a base plate, which is provided with screw-type elevating and traversing mechanisms to elevate/traverse the mortar. The M64 sight unit is attached to the bipod mount via a standard dovetail. An additional short-range sight is attached to the base of the cannon tube for firing the mortar on the move and during assaults. It has a spring-type shock absorber to absorb the shock of recoil in firing. The complete mortar weighs 46.5 pounds with an effective range out to 3,500 meters.

81mm Mortar

M252 81mm mortar is a medium extended-range indirect-fire weapon weighing in at ninety-one pounds. This

Soldiers from the 10th Mountain Division fire training mortar rounds from Forward Operating Base (FOB) Sharana, Afghanistan. The mortar provides long-range indirect-fire support to light infantry, air assault, and airborne units across the entire battalion front with sufficient range to engage targets out to the limit of the battalion zone of influence. *Sgt. Timothy Sander*

three-man-crew-served weapon is extremely accurate out to 5,700 meters. The muzzle end of the barrel has a short taper, which serves as a blast attenuator, and the breach end is finned for improved cooling. The M252 system consists of the M253 cannon (tube), M177 mortar mount, M3A1 baseplate, and M64A1 sight unit. The mortar provides long-range indirect fire support to light infantry, air assault, and airborne units across the entire battalion front, with sufficient range to engage targets out to the limit of the battalion zone of influence. It is capable of firing a variety of NATO-standard ammunition, including high-explosive, red phosphorous/smoke, and illumination.

Working out of Forward Operating Base (FOB) Bermel, Afghanistan, mortarmen of Company B, 2nd Battalion, 87th Infantry Regiment, 3rd BCT, 10th Mountain Division, demonstrate that the mortar is a key weapon on the battlefield. Although the heavy howitzers may be referred to as the king of artillery, the importance of the mortars and the crews cannot be overlooked regarding what they can bring to the battleground in the way of indirect fire support.

According to Staff Sgt. Brandon M. Alavarez, mortar section leader for Company B, 2nd Battalion, 87th Infantry Regiment, "Artillery is awesome; it's on target and it saves lives, but it's not as fast as a mortar. We provide immediate indirect fire for the company commander and the platoon leaders. While artillery has a greater range of fire and ammunition, the distance between the soldiers firing the artillery rounds and the troops in contact necessitates an extended process of coordination between the two groups. The mortarmen on the ground and in close contact with the commanders are able to provide support without the communication lag."

One of the advantages of the mortar over the fixed-position artillery is the fact that mortars were designed specifically to fire from one defilade position into another

The M198 155mm howitzer provides the artillerymen of the 10th Mountain Division with the destructive, suppressive, and protective indirect and direct field artillery fire in support of combined arms operations. U.S. soldiers from 6th Field Artillery Regiment, 10th Mountain Division, fire a round from a howitzer during training at the Warrior Range in Kirkuk, Iraq. *Spc. Laura M. Buchta*

defilade position. Such is often the case in Afghanistan when soldiers must engage Taliban or al Qaeda forces dug in on a mountainside or behind structures. In the rugged mountains of Afghanistan, the ability to shoot in such a manner is critical to combat operations. The mortar is often the quickest method of providing the soldiers on the ground with fast, accurate indirect-fire support. The mortar can often be used in close proximity to friendly forces, whereas heavy-artillery fire would be too dangerous to employ.

Sergeant David K. Kolk, a team leader with Company B, relates, "As a mortarman you can't make a mistake; if you make a mistake, you've just [killed friendly forces]. Our guys are extremely proficient; we have to be comfortable shooting up close. That's because when the training is done and the troops are in the field, they may be called on to shoot as close as fifty to one hundred meters from their fellow soldiers."

Staff Sergeant Alavarez recounts an event: "We were on the [Afghanistan-Pakistan] border and we were engaged by fifteen to twenty Taliban. Afterward, we were told that there was tracer fire going directly for the mortar team; it was aimed at us. The enemy had learned that mortar fire was an element of fire they wanted to quickly suppress. That let us know we are doing a good job. The company goes on a lot of dangerous missions, and they deserve the best support they can get."

M198 Towed Howitzer (155mm)

The M198 provides the artillerymen of the 10th Mountain Division with the destructive, suppressive, and protective indirect and direct field artillery fires in

Soldiers from 1st Platoon, Company C, 2nd Battalion, 87th Infantry Regiment, 3rd BCT, 10th Mountain Division, stop and survey the area during a convoy on March 22, 2007. Like most of the soldiers from 3rd BCT, 1st Platoon, they have spent more than fourteen months in Afghanistan. This up-armored HMMWV has glass around the turret called a Swanson shield; it is fitted in theater and was devised by the 1st BCT's 10th Mountain Division motor chief. *Spc. Matthew Leary*

support of combined arms operations. Commonly towed by a five-ton truck, the M198 system can also be dropped by parachute or transported by a CH-47 Chinook helicopter or C-130 aircraft.

The carriage of the M198 has a retractable suspension system and a top carriage that can be rotated 180 degrees to decrease overall length for shipment or storage. The fire control equipment may be used by one or two crewmen for either direct or indirect fire. The gunner on the left side controls left and right (traversing) settings, and the assistant gunner on the right side controls up and down (elevation) settings. The M198 will fire all current 155mm NATO-standard ammunition to include HE smoke, HC (hexachloroethane), and WP (white phosphorous); dual-purpose improved conventional munitions (DPICM); family of scatterable mines (FASCAM); cannon-launched guided projectiles (Copperhead); and illumination. Worth noting is the fact that the HE rounds weigh ninety-five pounds. The M198 has a crew of ten and an effective range out to 2,300 meters.

M998 High-Mobility Multipurpose Wheeled Vehicle (HMMWV)

The M998 high-mobility multipurpose wheeled vehicle (HMMWV) is a military four-wheel-drive (4WD) vehicle designed and manufactured by AM General. It was designed to replace the M151 one-quarter–ton military utility tactical truck (MUTT), the M561 "Gama Goat," as well as the M718A1 and M792 ambulance versions, the commercial utility cargo vehicle (CUCV), and other light trucks in service with the U.S. military. The HMMWV is also in service with various other

Lieutenant Colonel Gilbert, Commander of Task Force Irongray, 10th Mountain Division, from FOB Ghazni, supervises and watches as members of his task force and the Afghan National Police (not shown) maneuver into position to search a series of buildings for suspected insurgents near the town. The soldiers look through binoculars, scanning the area from their HMMWV with a mounted M240B machine gun. *Spc. Christopher Barnhardt*

countries and organizations. The vehicles are commonly referred to as Humvees or Hummers, though the latter term normally refers to the civilian-model sport utility vehicle (SUV) now manufactured by General Motors.

In June 1981, the army awarded AM General a contract for development of several prototype vehicles to be delivered to the U.S. government for a series of tests, and the company was later awarded the initial production contract for fifty-five thousand HMMWVs to be delivered in 1985. The HMMWVs first saw combat in Operation Just Cause, the U.S. invasion of Panama, in 1989. The HMMWV has become the vehicular backbone of U.S. forces around the world.

The HMMWV is built in a number of variations. The M998 is the baseline vehicle for the M998 series of 1.25-ton trucks, which are known as the HMMWV vehicles. The HMMWV vehicles include eleven variants. They are: M998 cargo/troop carrier; M1038 cargo/troop carrier, with winch; M1043 armament carrier; M1044 armament carrier, with winch; M1045 tow carrier; M1046 tow carrier, with winch; M997 ambulance, basic armor four-litter; M1035 ambulance, two-litter; M1037 shelter carrier; M1042 shelter carrier, with winch; and M1097 heavy HMMWV (payload of 4,400 pounds). All HMMWVs are designed for use on all types of roads, in all weather conditions, and are extremely effective in the most difficult terrain. The HMMWV's high power-to-weight ratio, four-wheel drive, and high ground clearance combine to give it outstanding cross-country mobility.

The HMMWV is 15 feet in length and 7 feet wide, with a height of 6 feet, which is reducible to 4.5 feet. Weighing in at 5,200 pounds, it is very capable of being airlifted by helicopter. The power plant is a V-8, 6.2-liter displacement, fuel-injected diesel, liquid-cooled with compression ignition. The HMMWV can ford just less than three feet of water without any preparation, and with the addition of a deep-water fording kit, it is capable of traversing through five feet of water. With a fuel capacity of twenty-five gallons, it gives the HMMWV a range of 350 highway miles with a cruising speed of up to sixty-five miles per hour.

As the U.S. military conducted missions in support of OEF and OIF, the soldiers encountered IED attacks on their vehicles. These IEDs could be as simple as an antivehicle mine or more elaborate and powerful explosives detonated by insurgents via various triggers, such as cell phones. The uses of demolitions are varied, because the insurgents place the devices in an assortment of ways. Some IEDs have been placed in old abandoned cars along the army's convoy route; other larger devices have been buried under roadways. Common placement of the IEDs was in positions to attack the soft sides of the HMMWV or the flat bottoms. Either method was extremely lethal and took its toll on U.S. and coalition forces.

It was clear to the soldiers on the ground and eventually to the war planners that the HMMWV was not designed for these types of attacks. HMMWVs were built for moving troops, not armored reconnaissance, convoy escort, and armed conflict in an urban environment; Mogadishu proved that point. In light of this threat, the soldiers did what good soldiers have done for centuries; they adapted and improvised. It became a common sight to see an HMMWV with boil-plates welded to the sides of the cargo compartment or doors. Piles of sandbags filled the cargo areas and interiors of the already cramped vehicles.

Eventually, the M998 would receive a substantial modification and would evolve into the M1114 up-armored HMMWV. Instead of building a new vehicle, the HMMWV received an assortment of added armor attached strategically around each vehicle. The modified M1114 provides soldiers with full 360-degree ballistic protection from IEDs, mine blasts, and overhead bursts. In addition to the new armor and anti-IED devices, the gunner's position is also modified to encapsulate the soldiers, protecting them from IEDs, small-arms fire, and even the occasional wire, which insurgents like to run across the streets at neck height.

M2 .50-Caliber Machine Gun

The Browning M2 .50-caliber machine gun has been serving American soldiers since the late twenties. Referred to as the "Ma Deuce" or simply the "fifty-cal," this heavy machine gun will definitely put "the fear of God" into any enemy. The M2 .50-caliber machine gun, heavy barrel is a crew-served, automatic, recoil-operated, air-cooled machine gun. It may be fed from either side by reconfiguring some of the component parts. A disintegrating metallic link belt is used to feed the ammunition into the weapon.

This gun has a back plate with spade grips, trigger, and bolt latch release. This gun may be mounted on ground mounts and most vehicles as an antipersonnel and antiaircraft weapon. The gun is equipped with a leaf-type rear sight, flash suppressor, and spare barrel assembly. Associated components are the M63 antiaircraft mount and the M3 tripod. The weapon is rather large with a length of sixty-two inches and weight of eighty-four pounds. The weapon has an effective range of two thousand meters with a maximum range of more than four miles.

MK19-3 40mm Grenade Machine Gun

The MK19 40mm machine gun is a self-powered, air-cooled, disintegrating, belt-fed, blowback-operated, fully automatic weapon. It is designed to deliver significant firepower against enemy personnel and lightly armored vehicles. It can be used in place of the M2 machine gun or to augment the heavy weapon.

The weapon fires a variety of 40mm grenades. The M430 HEDP 40mm grenade is capable of piercing up to two inches of armor and produces fragments to kill

Private First Class Matthew J. Mongiove, 10th Mountain Division, 4th Brigade, scans the area from the site of an M240 7.62mm machine gun, providing security in support of the 561st Military Police Company, 716th Military Police Battalion, 101st Airborne Division. Private First Class Mongiove supports the Canadian Mobile Training Team (MTT) as the Canadian Military Police teaches refresher training to the border patrol police guarding the borders of Afghanistan and Pakistan. *Sgt. Andre Reynolds*

personnel within five meters and wound personnel within fifteen meters of the point of impact. Other system components include: MK64 cradle mount, MOD 5; M3 tripod mount; and the AN/TVS-5 night vision sight. The complete weapon system weighs 175 pounds, with a rate of fire of 325 rounds per minute. The maximum range of the gun is 2,200 meters.

Global Positioning System (GPS)

The global positioning system (GPS) is a collection of satellites that orbit the earth twice a day. During this orbiting they transmit the precise time, latitude, longitude, and altitude information. Using a GPS receiver, the soldiers can ascertain their exact location anywhere on the earth.

The U.S. Department of Defense developed GPS in the early 1970s to provide a continuous, worldwide positioning and navigational system for U.S. military forces around the globe. The complete constellation, as it is referred to, consists of twenty-four satellites orbiting approximately twelve thousand miles above the earth. These twenty-two active and two reserve or backup satellites provide data twenty-four hours a day for 2D and 3D positioning anywhere on the planet. Each satellite constantly broadcasts precise time and location data. Troops using a GPS receiver receive these signals. The greater number of satellites and the more dynamic positions determine the person's location.

By measuring the time interval between the transmission of the satellite signal and the reception of the signal, the GPS receiver calculates the distance between the users and each satellite. Using the distance measurements of at least three satellites in an algorithm computation, the GPS receiver provides the precise location. Using a special encryption signal results in precise positioning service , which the military uses. A second signal called standard positioning service (SPS) is available for civilian and commercial uses.

Infantrymen use the Rockwell "Plugger," or PSN-11. The precise name for the unit is, PLGR+96 (precise lightweight GPS receiver). The PLGR+96 is the most advanced version of the U.S. Department of Defense handheld GPS unit.

Secure (Y-code) differential GPS (SDGPS) allows the user to accept differential correction without zeroing the unit. Differential accuracy can be less than one meter. Other features of the "Plugger" include wide area GPS enhancement for autonomous positioning accuracy to four meters circular error probable, jammer direction finding, targeting interface with laser range-finder, remote display terminal capability, and advanced user-interface features.

Weighing in at a mere 2.7 pounds (with batteries installed), the GPS unit is easily stowed in the rucksack or a MOLLE (modular lightweight load-carrying equipment) pouch. In addition to handheld operation, the PLGR+96 unit can be installed into various vehicles and airborne platforms.

Rappelling

Originating in the early days when the soldiers operated in the mountains, this old mountaineering technique still has its place in the modern infantryman's skill set. Whether working in mountainous terrain or in an urban environment, rappelling is a valuable skill.

The soldiers of the 10th Mountain Division train in this procedure with full combat gear. Attaching a regular military assault line through carabineers, or a specially designed rappelling device (known as "Figure 8"), the soldiers can negotiate down the side of a mountain like a mountain goat.

Iraqi army soldiers conduct a rappelling demonstration on the obstacle course at the 4th Brigade, 6th IA Division Commando Course graduation, held at Mahmudiyah, Iraq, on October 25, 2007. The three-week course trained the soldiers in advanced infantry tactics. Instructors were former graduates from the 4/6 IA. The course was originally designed and overseen by the 2nd Battalion, 15th Field Artillery Regiment, 2nd BCT, 10th Mountain Division. The course is modeled after the 10th Mountain Division pre-Ranger course.
Maj. Webster Wright

Chapter 5

AIRCRAFT

Soldiers from Company C, 2nd Battalion, 22nd Infantry Regiment, 1st BCT, 10th Mountain Division, and Iraqi soldiers are picked up in a UH-60 Black Hawk helicopter after completing an air assault mission southeast of Kirkuk. *Staff Sgt. Samuel Bendet*

UH-60 Black Hawk

The mission of the UH-60 is to provide air assault, general support, medical evacuation, command and control, and operational support to the division. The helicopter entered service with the army in 1979 as a replacement for the aging UH-1 series Bell Huey helicopters as a utility tactical transport helicopter. This versatile Black Hawk has enhanced the overall mobility of the division due to dramatic improvements in troop capacity and cargo lift capability. On the asymmetric battlefield, it provides the commander with the agility to get to the fight quicker and to mass effects throughout the battle space across the full spectrum of conflict. An entire fully equipped infantry squad can be lifted in a single Black Hawk and transported faster than in predecessor systems, in most weather conditions. The Black Hawk can airlift a 105mm howitzer, its crew, and up to thirty rounds of ammunition in a single lift. The aircraft's critical components and systems are armored or redundant, and its airframe is designed to progressively crush on impact to protect the crew and passengers.

A UH-60 from the 10th Combat Aviation Brigade (CAB) sits on the pad in Afghanistan in support of Operations Enduring Freedom. Operating in the mountainous terrain, the helicopters are a crucial weapon in the war on terror. *Courtesy 10th Mountain Division Public Affairs Office (PAO)*

OH-58 Kiowa Warrior

The Kiowa Warrior is rapidly deployable by air and can be fully operational within minutes of arrival. Two Kiowa aircraft can be transported in a C-130 aircraft. For air transportation the vertical tailfin pivots, the main rotor blades and the horizontal stabilizer are folded, and the mast mounted site, the IFF antenna, and the lower wire cutter are removed. The landing gear can also be lowered to decrease the height of the aircraft.

The mission of the OH-58 helicopter is to conduct armed reconnaissance, security, target acquisition and designation, command and control, light attack, and defensive air-combat missions in support of combat and contingency operations. The Kiowa Warrior replaced the AH-1 Cobra attack helicopter, which had functioned as the scout helicopter for air-cavalry troops and light-attack companies. Entering service with the army in 1991, the Kiowa is a single-engine, four-bladed helicopter with advanced navigation, communication, and weapons and cockpit integration systems.

The mast-mounted sight houses a thermal imaging system, low-light television, laser range-finder/designator, and an optical bore sight system. These systems enable the Kiowa Warrior to operate in both day and night environments and allow target acquisition and engagement at standoff ranges and in adverse-weather conditions. The highly accurate navigation system of the OH-58 provides precise target location that can be sent digitally to other aircraft or artillery via advanced digital communications systems. Battlefield imagery can also be transmitted to provide near-real-time situational awareness to command and control elements. The laser designator can provide autonomous designation for the Laser Hellfire or remote designation for other laser-guided precision weapons.

The Kiowa Warrior is equipped with two universal quick-change weapons pylons. Each pylon can be armed with two Hellfire missiles, seven Hydra 70 rockets, two air-to-air Stinger missiles, or one .50-caliber fixed forward machine gun. The armament systems combine to provide antiarmor, antipersonnel, and antiaircraft capabilities at standoff ranges.

While the remainder of the 10th Mountain Division went to Afghanistan, the 1/10th Attack Battalion had

A Black Hawk helicopter takes on fuel at a forward arming and refueling point (FARP). Using FARPs, the aircrews can decrease their turnaround time, which is critical in supply missions, as well as in inserting and extracting troops from the battlefield. *Courtesy 10th Mountain Division PAO*

Flying over Afghanistan's lush green fields, the gunner of this UH-60 keeps a watchful eye for any enemy forces. This Black Hawk helicopter is armed with two M240 7.62mm machine guns mounted on each side of the helicopter. *Courtesy 10th Mountain Division PAO*

been attached to the 101st Combat Aviation Brigade in support of Task Force Band of Brothers. The task force patrols northern Iraq where the Kiowas can be utilized to patrol the city streets of Mosul.

The OH-58D is being used for numerous missions in support of OIF. According to Maj. David Bingham, the executive officer for the 1/10th Attack Aviation Battalion, "Originally, it looked like we'd replace 2nd Battalion, 101st Combat Aviation Brigade, in Key West, Iraq. They were in direct support of the 172nd Stryker Brigade there. We skipped the usual stop at Kuwait and flew straight to Q-West. At the time, the big focus was on the elections in the December 2005 time frame. Then the assets became needed elsewhere. For a while, we were split in three locations and had forward arming and refueling points operating here in Mosul, as well as in

Q-West. The battalion started arriving in Mosul in October and was split into two areas of operation. The pilots have logged roughly seventeen thousand hours in and around Mosul. The battalion also has a company at FOB Sykes near Tall'Afar, Iraq, which patrols the area there as part of Task Force No Mercy with 1st Battalion, 101st Combat Aviation Brigade."

During their initial deployment to Iraq, the 1/10th Attack Battalion, known as the "Dragon" battalion, flew OH-58D Kiowa Warrior armed reconnaissance helicopters to patrol the Mosul area along with AH-64 Apache attack helicopters of 2nd Battalion, 101st Combat Aviation Brigade. In concert, these two aircraft operated in what is referred to as "pink teams." This old term originated in the Vietnam War era in which an attack aircraft flies high above a target area while the scout helicopter maneuvers lower, using its capabilities to watch for insurgents in the urban environment. Once the scout helicopter identifies a target, the AH-64 can swoop down for the kill.

The pilots of the 1/10th will fly a few hundred feet off the deck during day and night. When they spot suspicious activity, they can call in the Apaches, or in this

Dealing with the enemy is one thing, but when you have to fight nature as well, it can be downright frustrating. Here a dust storm fully engulfs the flight line of UH-60 helicopters in Iraq. The fine talcum powder–like sand scratches the windscreens and permeates every part of the aircraft. *U.S. Army photo*

U.S. Army Specialist Richard Dietz from Company A, 7th Battalion, 158th Aviation Regiment, keeps watch in a CH-47 Chinook helicopter over eastern Afghanistan. *Staff Sgt. Michael L. Casteel*

U.S. Army Staff Sergeant Clint Ezell from Company A, 7th Battalion, 158th Aviation Regiment, keeps watch from the tailgate of a CH-47 Chinook helicopter over eastern Afghanistan. Mounted to the rear of the helicopter is an M2 .50-caliber machine gun. *Staff Sgt. Michael L. Casteel*

U.S. Army soldiers from 10th CAB, 10th Mountain Division, refuel a CH-47 Chinook helicopter in Naray, Afghanistan. *Staff Sgt. Marcus J. Quarterman*

case, ground elements of the 172nd Stryker Brigade who are patrolling the city.

Working in direct support of the 172nd Stryker Brigade, the 1/10th will execute a variety of missions in the Mosul area. As a pilot with Company A of the Dragons, Chief Warrant Officer Two Steve Workman remarked, "I loved it [flying in pink teams]. We have a pure gunship above us. What better thing is there to cover us? Being there for the ground guys is really what it's about for us. If there's a patrol in the city, we want to be overhead and support those guys no matter what they're doing. If they're waiting on the explosive ordnance team to show up to remove an improvised explosive device (IED), we'll stay overhead and support those guys. We still get a few deliberate missions like cordon and searches or cordon and knocks throughout the week. Or if not much is going on, we might be doing route recons."

"We (1/10th and the 172nd) have a pretty good relationship," said Chief Warrant Officer Three Dean Leasure, an Alpha Company maintenance test pilot. "They like us being overhead when they are on the ground and especially when they're dismounted, and we like them on the ground when we're flying around. It is a mutually supporting relationship that increases the effectiveness and security of both of the combat systems."

The 1/10th pilots said much of their work is similar to policeman on patrol; there is no "average" day. Company A pilot 1st Lt. Jared Sutton remarked, "We kind of live for that ten or fifteen minutes of excitement when the ground guys call us up with something to do. You get pumped up to help them out."

Major Bingham said, "The Kiowas will provide security for convoys. If a vehicle breaks down, the Kiowa is on hand to provide security from above. The Kiowa will also look for suspicious activity on the ground, such as people digging or weighted-down vehicles, as well as suspicious things that could be IEDs and call them in to the Stryker brigade below. They have found several IEDs this way. Mosul's the second largest city in Iraq, with a population of around 1.8 million people. There's a lot of clutter in the city, so it's a challenging task looking for things that aren't supposed to be there. During IED attacks, the Kiowa teams will look for the triggerman responsible.

Apaches Rescue Cavalry

In the summer of 2007, Chief Warrant Officers Mark Burrows and Steven Cianfrini with the 17th Cavalry Regiment's Troop C, 3rd Squadron, took off from their base in Iraq. What began as a routine reconnaissance mission with a sister scout helicopter would turn into a life-or-death situation for the two OH-58 Kiowa pilots.

The aviators were supporting an infantry unit south of Baghdad and had just located a suspected roadside improvised explosive device (IED). Chief Warrant Officer Cianfrini was the first to spot the enemy fire as tracers reached out to the OH-58 from the ground below. Cianfrini immediately called out to Chief Warrant Officer Burrows to evade the incoming rounds. As the small-arms fire ceased, the pilots made the decision to return to base and assess any damage. All of a sudden, a heavy machine gun opened up on the small scout helicopter. Large caliber rounds began to impact the vulnerable Kiowa over and over. There was no time to locate and engage the enemy with the aircraft's weapons. The pilots bobbed and weaved as best they could to avoid the incoming rounds.

Chief Warrant Officer Cianfrini recalled, "I saw the tracer rounds come up through the rotors, and at that point we tried to get out of range, check our instruments, make sure our systems were good and that nobody was hit." As they continued to evade the enemy fire, several rounds from the machine gun found their mark. Slamming into the aircraft, the cockpit was abuzz with warning alarms and warning lights. More rounds hit the aircraft and destroyed the instrument panel. Chief Warrant Officer Cianfrini related, "One second it was there; the next it was a mess of wires."

Having suffered multiple hits by both small- and large-caliber munitions, which caused extensive damage to the helicopter, the pilots knew they were going down. Chief Warrant Officer Burrows stated, "From the time the second engagement started to when we hit the ground, we were taking fire the whole time."

The damaged Kiowa shook strongly as Chief Warrant Officer Burrows made the decision to attempt a controlled landing in a nearby field. He maneuvered the stricken helicopter back and forth in an attempt to escape the intense ground fire. Getting closer to the ground, he began to slow the OH-58, only to have the aircraft start spinning. At this point he knew his tail rotor had been hit and was of no use. He continued his autorotation in an effort to cushion the landing. Nevertheless, the Kiowa came down hard, bounced over a canal, and came to rest near a roadway, settling on its left side.

Aviators say any landing you can walk away from is a good landing. This was the case with the two chiefs. The pilots were banged up, bruised, and scratched but otherwise uninjured. They hurriedly climbed out of the helicopter and met near the front of the downed aircraft. Evaluating their current situation, Chief Warrant Officer Cianfrini realized his M4 carbine had been tossed from the aircraft when they hit the ground. The enemy, having located the downed Kiowa, again opened fire on the American aviators.

The two pilots agreed it was time to put some distance between them and the enemy. Making their way into the canal, the pilots utilized the dense growth of reeds to camouflage themselves. Chief Warrant Officer Burrows related, "When we got into it, we realized the water was up to our necks and we were in knee-deep mud. We physically couldn't move from the center of the canal." This predicament actually turned into a favorable position for the pilots. Had they not gotten stuck in the canal and continued up the other bank, they would have run into another group of insurgents. The enemy soldiers, now gathered on both banks of the canal, began shooting blindly into the reeds.

Concealed in the reeds, Chief Warrant Officer Burrows remembers that moment: "All we could do was wait for what seemed to be the inevitable. Bullets clipped the reeds around us, hitting the water we were standing in but not us. They just didn't see us. I had one of the attackers in my sights, but I knew if I'd shot him they would have known where we were."

Not having any success with their assault rifles, the insurgents pulled up to the canal in a truck and began firing into the reeds with a heavy machine gun. Again, the rounds came close but none of them hit the pilots who had hunkered down in the water. Eventually, the insurgents gave up the hunt, loaded into their trucks, and left the area. Chief Warrant Officer Burrows commented, "When they started leaving, walking away, I felt amazement that we were still there."

The other Kiowa that had been flying with Chief Warrant Officer Burrows had also come under enemy fire. As they moved off to a safer distance, they radioed in for reinforcements. In response to Chief Warrant Officer Burrows' radio call, "Fallen Angel," indicating a coalition aircraft had gone down, army helicopters and air force jets began arriving on the scene.

A pair of AH-64 Apaches from the 1st Cavalry Division, Fort Hood, Texas, responded to Chief Warrant Officer Burrows' distress call and was orbiting nearby. One of the Apaches, piloted by Chief Warrant Officers Allan Davison and Micah Johnson, landed near the downed pilots. Chief Warrant Officer Johnson, the front-seat pilot, jumped out to check Chief Warrant Officers Burrows and Cianfrini for injuries.

There was a real concern the insurgents may return to engage the aircraft rescuing their comrades. To expedite the extraction of the downed pilots, the decision was made not to wait for a Black Hawk or other type of helicopter. The pilots would be extracted using a technique called the "spur ride." This method, though rather unorthodox, was a practical and functional means of removing the pilots from harm's way. Chief Warrant Officers Burrows and Cianfrini climbed up on the stubby wings of the AH-64 helicopter. These wings, located on both sides of the aircraft, were used to hold the weapons stores, that is, AGM-114 Hellfire missiles, folding-fin rocket pods, and so forth. Using their safety harnesses and D-rings, the pair of Kiowa pilots attached themselves to the exterior of the airframe. Secured to the Apache helicopter, the gunship pilot lifted off and returned to base with his passengers.

Thirty minutes had elapsed from the crash landing to their rescue. Chief Warrant Officer Burrows stated, "It wasn't the most comfortable flight, but I was elated to be out of there. I knew we would be rescued, but I can't believe that through all this we made it through without serious injury. That's the kind of unbelievable part." Chief Warrant Officer Cianfrini added, "It happened so fast I don't think we really thought about much except just trying to stay alive."

An OH-58D Kiowa Warrior helicopter takes off from Mosul Airfield in Iraq. *Capt. Scott M. Betts*

Just the presence of a Kiowa in the air will stifle many possible attacks."

"Us being overhead is a huge factor," said Company A pilot Chief Warrant Officer Two Brian Parks. "The enemy really doesn't do a whole lot when we're overhead. The ground guys will tell us they're taking fire, and as soon as we roll over top of them, it's done."

The battalion conducts a variety of missions. On one day the 1/10th pilots may be in the air in support of military police units and coalition training advisers who work with the Iraqi Army (IA) and Iraqi police. Another day, the pilots may be providing security for a medical evacuation helicopter transporting wounded soldiers to a treatment facility, according to Lieutenant Sutton.

AH-64 Apache

The AH-64 Apache is the army's heavy division/corps attack helicopter. The AH-64D Longbow remanufacture effort incorporates a millimeter-wave fire control radar (FCR), radar frequency interferometer (RFI), fire-and-forget radar-guided Hellfire missile and cockpit management, and digitization enhancements. The combination of the FCR, RFI, and the advanced navigation and avionics suite of the aircraft provide increased situational awareness, lethality, and survivability. The mission of the AH-64D is to conduct rear and close missions and deep precision strikes. The helicopter can also be tasked to provide armed reconnaissance when required in day and night environments, obscured-battlefield situations, and adverse-weather conditions. The

Pilots Chief Warrant Officer Two Steve Workman (left) and Chief Warrant Officer Two Brian V. Parks(right) both of Company A, 1st Battalion, 10th Aviation Regiment, position their M4 rifles in the cockpit of their Kiowa Warrior OH-58D armed reconnaissance helicopter prior to a flight over the city of Mosul, Iraq. The battalion has logged more than seventeen thousand hours flying over Mosul in support of the 172nd Stryker BCT since October 2005. *Capt. Scott M. Betts*

Longbow has a crew of two, a pilot and copilot/gunner. It is armed with AGM-114 Hellfire missiles, 2.75-inch folding-fin rockets, and a M230 30mm chain gun.

CH-47 Chinook

The Chinook is the largest helicopter in the division's inventory. Its mission is to transport ground forces, supplies, ammunition, and other mission-critical cargo in support of worldwide combat and contingency operations. The large helicopter entered service with the army in 1962 and has proven itself time and time again. Whether in the jungles of Vietnam or the mountains of Afghanistan, the Chinook is the workhorse of the aviation brigade. The CH-47 is a twin-engine, tandem-rotor helicopter that has undergone several iterations and upgrades since the first CH-47A model was delivered to the army for use in Vietnam. Beginning in 1982 and ending in 1994, all CH-47A, B, and C models were upgraded to the CH-47D version. The D model is currently the U.S. Army standard and features composite rotor blades, an improved electrical system, modularized hydraulics, triple cargo hooks, avionics and communication improvements, and more powerful engines that can handle a 19,500-pound load—nearly twice the Chinook's original lift capacity. An upgrade program exists to remanufacture 300 of the current fleet of 435 CH-47Ds to the CH-47F standard.

An OH-58D Kiowa Warrior helicopter lands on the FARP on Mosul Airfield in Iraq. *Capt. Scott M. Betts*

Chief Warrant Officer Brian V. Parks, a Kiowa pilot with the Company A ("Rogues"), 2nd Battalion, 10th Aviation Regiment, prepares for a flight over Mosul, Iraq, on Mosul Airfield. Chief Warrant Officer Parks has clipped two thirty-round magazines together, as well as a third magazine attached to the RIS. *Capt. Scott M Betts*

The Chinook's cockpit accommodates two pilots and an observer. The communications suite includes jam-resistant high-frequency and ultrahigh-frequency radio systems, and the helicopter is equipped with an identification friend or foe interrogator. Three machine guns can be mounted on the helicopter, two in the crew door on the starboard side and one window-mounted on the port side. In a defensive mode, the helicopter is equipped with a suite of countermeasure systems, which could include one or more of the following: a missile approach warning device, jamming equipment, radar warning devices, and chaff and flare dispensers.

The Chinook has a triple hook system that provides stability to large external loads or the capacity for multiple external loads. Large external loads such as 155mm howitzers can be transported at speeds up to 260 kilometers per hour using the triple-hook load configuration. Multiple external loads can be delivered to two or three separate destinations in one sortie.

The cabin provides forty-two cubic meters of cargo space and twenty-one square meters of cargo floor area and can accommodate two HMMWVs or one HMMWV together with a 105mm howitzer and gun crew. The main cabin can hold up to thirty-three fully equipped troops. When configured for medical evacuation, the cabin can accommodate twenty-four litters.

The Chinook is powered by two turbo-shaft engines, which are pod-mounted on either side of the rear pylon under the rear rotor blades. The self-sealing fuel tanks are mounted in external fairings on the sides of the fuselage. The fixed tanks hold 1,030 gallons of fuel. Three additional fuel tanks can be carried in the cargo area.

The CH-47F upgrade program will involve the installation of a new digital cockpit and modifications to the airframe to reduce vibration. The upgraded cockpit will provide future growth potential and will include a digital data bus that permits installation of enhanced communications and navigation equipment for improved situational awareness, mission performance, and survivability. Airframe structural modifications will reduce harmful vibrations, reducing operations and support costs and improving crew endurance. Other airframe modifications will reduce the time required for aircraft teardown and buildup after deployment on a C-5 or C-17 by nearly sixty percent.

A separate but complementary effort involves the installation of the more powerful and reliable, Honeywell 55-GA-714A engine, which improves fuel efficiency and enhances lift performance by approximately 3,900

Soldiers refuel and arm an awaiting Kiowa Warrior helicopter at the 2nd Squadron, 17th Cavalry Regiment Sabre FARP on FOB Warrior in Kirkuk, Iraq.
Sgt. Ryan Matson

Chief Warrant Officers Mark Burrows (left) and Steven Cianfrini of the 17th Cavalry Regiment's Troop C, 3rd Squadron, were rescued by an AH-64 Apache helicopter after their helicopter, an OH-58D Kiowa, was shot down. *Sgt. 1st Class Thomas Mills*

A U.S. Army AH-64D Apache Longbow helicopter, armed with AGM-114 Hellfire air-to-ground missiles and 2.75-inch rocket pods, is in flight during a test conducted at the Boeing/McDonnell Douglas facility, located near Mesa, Arizona. *Master Sgt. Lance Cheung*

pounds (enabling it to carry the M198 155mm towed howitzer). Installation of an improved crash-worthy extended-range fuel system (ERFS II) will enable Chinook self-deployment and extend the operational radius of all other missions.

3/71st Establishes Firebases

Members of the 3/71st Cavalry served in the northern region of Afghanistan in the Nuristan Province, where they established a firebase in the village of Kamu near Kamdesh as part of Task Force Spartan. Cavalry elements continued to press their operations into the northernmost area of the eastern Afghan battle space. Firebase Camp Keating was built with the purpose of blocking enemy activity along the Kamdesh road. It is estimated that the firebase is one of the most austere camps established in the northern sector of Regional Command East.

"The site, just north of the village of Kamu, is set right between Kamdesh and Bazgahl," related Sgt. 1st Class Jason Burch, 3rd Platoon, A Troop, 3/71st Cavalry.

An AH-64 Apache helicopter from 10th CAB, 10th Mountain Division, refuels in Jalalabad, Afghanistan. *Staff Sgt. Marcus J. Quarterman*

A U.S. Army AH-64 Apache attack helicopter lands with the sun low over Camp Cook (Taji), Salah ad Din, Iraq, during Operation Iraqi Freedom.
Tech. Sgt. Russell E. Cooley IV

"In the past, every time we rolled out of the gate, we were pretty sure we were going to get shot at. We were also losing a lot of supplies along the route due to the enemy ransacking our jinga trucks." A *jinga* truck is a large flat-bed vehicle indigenous to the region, used for the transportation of various supplies. They are most commonly adorned with bright colors and an assortment of brass bells, chimes, and other accouterments, which earned them the nickname *jingle truck*, which the troops have morphed to just *jinga*.

The site of the firebase was initially occupied by Afghan National Army (ANA) soldiers and a team of embedded trainers. It has since been reinforced by a platoon-sized element from Task Force Titan. U.S.

Army First Lieutenant Chris York, leader, 3rd Platoon, A Troop, 3/71st Cavalry said, "Our objective is to provide a highly visible presence. Our presence in Kamu is an added effect to the major operations the ANA are executing along the Kamdesh road. We are essentially there to support the ANA, to provide stronger firepower for them if needed. ANA soldiers have grown increasingly sure-handed in their security efforts along the Kamdesh road. The [ANA] set up regular checkpoints along the road. They also execute mounted and dismounted patrols in the area."

The Kamu area proved an excellent place to set up operations for Task Force Titan soldiers and Afghans alike. The local populace of Kamu benefited as well as the Afghan National Security Forces. Lieutenant York related, "The site is visible from the village of Kamu. We are better able to provide village assessments and work with the locals because of our more available position. We are right next to the town, so we have more ready access to the elders. We have and will continue to bring jobs to the people of Kamu. We employ them to build makeshift structures during our stay on the Kamu site, and they also help run supplies back from Camp Keating. The difference is substantial. The ambushes against our convoys and even the local nationals have definitely tapered off. Once the enemy realizes we are not going anywhere for a while, they give up. Key leaders have assessed the area. The battlefield is an ever-shifting puzzle. The ultimate decision is still in the air, but for now, we are providing the type of support Afghan forces need right now."

This region of Afghanistan had been a hot spot for many years; yet, today it has begun to settle down due to the exhaustive efforts of Task Force Titan soldiers and their Afghan counterparts. Their hold on the areas of Kamdesh and Kamu are currently stronger than it has ever been. Leaders said they hope those trends continue, allowing the Afghan government an opportunity to take deep roots in the province of Nuristan.

CH-47s—Airlift Beans, Bullets, and Bandages

One thing you will not see in the mountainous northern region of Afghanistan is a vast infrastructure of paved highways. Roads have been worn into the mountains by years of goat carts, lorries, Soviet armor, local jinga trucks, and, most recently, the U.S. military. Traveling through these rudimentary roads by HMMWV is often an invitation to ambush from the high ground. Such an environment is a daunting challenge for any logistician. Army Staff Sergeant George Beckett, logistics noncommissioned officer in charge, Company C, 3/71st Cavalry related, "Without roads developed in these mountain regions, it's difficult to get supplies out to the combat operation areas."

According to Capt. Jeffrey O'Dell, operations commander for the 3/71st Cavalry, "The soldiers from Company C, 3rd Squadron, 71st Cavalry Regiment, 10th Mountain Division, carry out movements throughout the northeastern region of Afghanistan and rely on Task Force Pegasus to provide provisions and transportation to their mission locations."

Supplies including ammunition, food, water, mail, and combat equipment are transported in CH-47 Chinooks by means of sling-loading cargo underneath the aircraft or packing the aircraft's body with troops and supplies. A CH-47 can carry up to ten thousand pounds of cargo in one trip. Staff Sergeant Beckett related, "Task Force Pegasus transports supplies almost weekly, keeping our soldiers well equipped and satisfied. If we don't receive a delivery of water, soldiers don't drink water. Aviation support is that essential."

U.S. Army Sergeant David Fischer, fire squad leader, Company C, 3/71st Cavalry, said, "Whether it is mail, ammunition, or food packs, whenever a resupply helicopter arrives, especially before a mission, our team's entire attitude changes for the better. Getting mail out here is like Christmas day."

Chapter 6

GLOBAL WAR ON TERRORISM

Soldiers of the 10th Mountain Division work in tandem with Iraqi army (IA) forces to detain suspects. Working closely with the IA soldiers gives the mountain infantrymen the advantage of having local forces who know the culture, language, and people. *Staff Sgt. Samuel Bendet*

On September 11, 2001, the United States was attacked by Islamofascists as they hijacked commercial airliners and converted them into missiles. These cowardly thugs were successful in hitting the World Trade Center in New York and the Pentagon in Washington D.C. These heinous actions created ripples throughout the civilized world as freedom-loving people condemned the attacks. Closer to home, the impact of this evil was felt three hundred miles northwest of ground zero at Fort Drum, New York, the home of the 10th Mountain Division.

Operation Enduring Freedom

1st Brigade Combat Team

The soldiers of the 1st BCT would be one of the first conventional army units to be deployed in support of Operation Enduring Freedom (OEF). Within a month after the terrorist attacks, on October 5, 2001, Task Force 1/87th Infantry deployed to Karsi Khanabad Airfield, Uzbekistan. Referred to as K2, the site was an old Soviet airbase that had become the home of Camp Stronghold Freedom. The Task Force consisted of soldiers from the 1/87th Infantry, 3/6th Field Artillery, 3/62nd Antiaircraft Defense Artillery, 110th Military Intelligence, and Air Support Operation Squadron, U.S. Air Force.

During the month of November 2001, the 1st Battalion, 87th Infantry deployed to Bagram Airfield, Afghanistan, where they provided security and support for combat missions. The soldiers of the 87th Infantry would also participate in Operation Anaconda, where they would conduct combat operations in the Lower Shah-e-kot Valley, Afghanistan. After a highly successful

At Naval Air Station Sigonella, Italy, members of Company B, 1st Battalion, 87th Infantry Regiment, 10th Mountain Division, board a C-17A Globemaster III for a forward deployment as part of Operation Enduring Freedom. *Staff Sgt. Ken Bergmann*

deployment, the task force returned to Fort Drum, New York, in April 2002.

In July 2003, the mountain soldiers of the 1st Battalion, 87th Infantry, returned to Afghanistan for OEF IV. The Soldiers of 1/87th conducted combat and humanitarian assistance operations from frontline firebases in Gardez, Shkin, Orgun-E, and Khowst. The battalion also operated in the remote region of Paktika province, frequently patrolling at altitudes above eight thousand feet. The 1/87th Infantry continually worked to improve the conditions throughout the Paktika province. The battalion improved the security and stability in the region. The 1st Battalion, 87th Infantry, returned to Fort Drum, New York, in April 2004, after destroying Taliban and al Qaeda forces in the their area of operation and improving the security and quality of life for the local populace.

2nd Brigade Combat Team

During the time between July 2001 and January 2003, the 2nd BCT was deployed to Afghanistan in support of the Global War on Terrorism (GWOT). The brigade headquarters deployed from December 2001 through April 2002 for OEF in Afghanistan. Second battalion, 14th Infantry, and 2nd Battalion, 87th Infantry, conducted peacekeeping operations in Kosovo and the Sinai, respectively. Fourth battalion, 31st Infantry, deployed forces to Afghanistan, Uzbekistan, Kuwait, and Qatar.

From May to December 2003, the brigade headquarters and 4/31st Infantry deployed to Afghanistan in support of OEF as part of the coalition joint Task Force Phoenix. The mountain soldiers were responsible for training the Afghan National Army (ANA). From July 2003 to August 2004, the 2/87th Infantry were

Soldiers in 3rd Platoon, Combat Company, 1st Battalion, 32nd Infantry Regiment, climb into the snowline of a mountain near the village of Aybat in eastern Afghanistan during a two-week-long mission, which included patrols, air assaults, and talks with the local elders to establish a link between the local populace and the Afghan government. *Spc. Jon Arguello*

deployed to Afghanistan in support of OEF to fight the GWOT.

10th Sustainment Brigade

Since October 2001, 10th DISCOM units have continually deployed to both Afghanistan and Iraq in support of OEF and OIF. They have set new standards for combat service support and exceeded every one of them, including providing support to the 101st Airborne Division (Air Assault), the 3rd Infantry Division, and the newly constituted Afghan National Army. During this period, the 10th DISCOM headquarters itself deployed to Afghanistan for OEF IV to serve as the Joint Logistics Command for the Combined/Joint Task Force 180. Upon return, the 10th DISCOM immediately began to transform to meet the new army requirements. The 10th DISCOM transformed into the 10th Support Brigade Troops Battalion and the 548th Corps Support Battalion.

Throughout a wide range of operations over the course of many years and in every climate, the Muleskinners have provided support to combat units by pack mule or truck, ice axe or forklift. During their short history, the soldiers of the 10th DISCOM have excelled at providing, sustaining, and treating the soldiers of the 10th Mountain Division with world-class logistics support in supply, maintenance, medical, and transportation operations while being able to step back from the "Trains" to fight and win along side the division. Today, the Muleskinners continue their standard of climbing to glory and supporting the climb the entire way.

Soldiers of Company B, 1st Battalion, 32nd Infantry Regiment, 10th Mountain Division, led by members of the ANA move through the mountainside village of Aranas while on patrol in the Nuristan province of Afghanistan. *Spc. Eric Jungels*

3rd Brigade Combat Team

Just after daybreak in March 2007, soldiers of the 1st Platoon, Company C, 2nd Battalion, 87th Infantry Regiment, 3rd BCT, 10th Mountain Division, embarked on their mission from FOB Orgun-E, Afghanistan. What started off as a routine patrol would end up lasting more than thirteen hours. In addition to the platoon, the soldiers were accompanied by another member of the patrol, Mr. Murphy.

While traveling to an isolated outpost where they were to deliver supplies, the convoy was stuck in a traffic jam when several of the local civilian vehicles became stuck in the mud. Clearing the mud and locals, the soldiers of the 2/87th continued with their mission and delivered the needed supplies. On the return trip to the FOB, Mr. Murphy put in another appearance, as two of the convoy vehicles had mechanical breakdowns, one of which required exhaustive repair. To further complicate matters, the sun had set, the light had faded, and the weather began to turn cold.

Sergeant Jordan Ansley, a team leader in 3rd Squad, 1st Platoon, remarked, "It's Murphy's Law. Anything that

Soldiers of Company B, 1st Battalion, 32nd Infantry Regiment, 10th Mountain Division, move through the mountainside village of Aranas while on patrol. *Spc. Eric Jungels*

can go wrong will go wrong." While a visit from Mr. Murphy on the battlefield is nothing new, it seemed to the soldiers of the 3rd BCT that he was making more than his fair share of appearances when the entire brigade received orders that their tour would be extended. In January 2007, the 4th BCT, 82nd Airborne Division, began deploying to Afghanistan to replace the soldiers of the 3rd BCT, 10th Mountain Division, who were completing a yearlong deployment. The Department of Defense (DoD) then announced an increased force structure plan for Regional Command East. The results of this news meant instead of one brigade covering the area, two brigades would split the battle space, doubling the combat effectiveness within the region. This also meant the soldiers of the 2/87th Infantry and the rest of 3rd BCT, 10th Mountain Division, would stay in Afghanistan for an extra four months until relieved by the 173rd Airborne Brigade.

The surprise news of the extension hit a lot of soldiers hard at first, but according to Sgt. Craig Putnam, a squad automatic weapon's gunner with 3rd Squad, "The soldiers of 1st Platoon, Company C, quickly rallied together and focused on the mission at hand. We've been through worse. Being here a little extra time didn't make that much of a difference. Nothing goes exactly as planned, so this was no different."

"The extension was a perfect example of Murphy's Law in action," Sgt. Ansley said. But the soldiers grouped together and made the best of the situation, keeping unit morale high. The soldiers of Company C carried on with their missions of conducting patrols and going out on convoy support. As a result of the DoD extension, many of the 10th Mountain Division soldiers would serve more than four hundred consecutive days in a combat zone. Sergeant First Class Gonzalo Lassally, 1st Platoon sergeant, said, "I think they handled it better than most. Everyone probably thinks that their platoon is the best, so I am not going to say they're the best, but they are the tightest."

As the soldiers who have fought in the countless wars before them, the soldiers of this generation became their own "band of brothers." The bond formed by soldiers in a combat environment is one those in the civilian world can never equal. Sergeant Lassally confirmed, "I don't think anybody would have gone back home unless the whole platoon went home. They are like family to one

This photo gives you an idea of how rugged and expansive the environment is that U.S. soldiers have to maneuver in. A soldier (near center) from Company B, 1st Battalion, 32nd Infantry Regiment, 10th Mountain Division, negotiates the mountainous terrain of the Nuristan province while on patrol. *Spc. Eric Jungels*

another. Amazingly, considering what they have been put through, they are still reenlisting. We are at a ninety percent reenlistment with seventy percent of that being to stay in the unit." Although these soldiers are separated from loved ones, family, and friends, they understand their mission is important, and they carry on in spite of the hardships. This is what soldiers do and while serving their county is a vital mission, it remains that they are in reality serving one another.

A prime example of this bond is Sgt. Mark T. Clinger, an antiarmor specialist with the platoon who served in 1st Platoon for more than three years and two deployments to Afghanistan. In 2004, while deployed with 1st Platoon to Afghanistan, Sergeant Clinger was injured in an IED attack. The attack killed one of his fellow platoon members and sent him to the hospital for several months. Today, the permanent scars on his left forearm and above his right eye constantly remind Sergeant Clinger of the attack that almost took his life. In spite of all this, he drives on. Sergeant Clinger said, "These younger guys need someone who has been through it to kind of show them the way; so that's why I reenlisted. I've reenlisted twice now."

As darkness envelops FOB Orgun-E, the soldiers of 1st Platoon, Company C, 2/87th Infantry, return. They know all too well that tomorrow will bring another mission; yet they do what soldiers have done through the ages: grab some chow and get some sack time. As they prepare for their next mission, they will clean their weapons, service their vehicles, and refit for the task at hand, all the while laughing and joking with one another as they conduct this dangerous thing called war.

Sergeant Ansley said, "Just as the convoy returned back to FOB Orgun-E later than expected, the soldiers will

Major Douglas Sloan, company commander, Company B, 1st Battalion, 32nd Infantry Regiment, 10th Mountain Division, confirms information provided by locals with an Afghan interpreter while on patrol in Aranas. *Spc. Eric Jungels*

return home to Fort Drum, New York, a little later than expected. And although both missions ran long, the soldiers of 1st Platoon carry on with a high level of morale and camaraderie." U.S. Army First Lieutenant William L. Felder, 1st Platoon Leader, Company C, further commented, "They have taken [the extension] well. There are things everyone wants to go home for, but they know it's mission first. Murphy's Law will affect only their timetable; it will not affect the platoon's spirit or commitment to the mission. The platoon is capable of handling any other unexpected thing thrown its way. If we get extended again, we'll do the best job we can," he said. "And that's the bottom line."

Vikings Earn Their Mountain Tab

Conducting missions out of Jalalabad Airfield, Afghanistan, soldiers from Task Force Spartan demonstrated that they live up to their brigade's historical lineage and namesake. These soldiers, who operated in one of the harshest environments in the world, earned every letter in the 10th Mountain Division's mountain tab. After two weeks of patrolling, climbing, and searching the mountains and valleys in eastern Afghanistan, infantrymen from 3rd Platoon, Company C, 1st Battalion 32nd Infantry Regiment, demonstrated the determination and spirit to pursue the enemy until the very last day of their deployment. These soldiers, who wore mountain tabs above crossed bayonets on their shoulder patch, demonstrated they were undaunted by the rough terrain, oppressive heat, muddy snow-capped mountains, or their extended deployments.

On "Operation Big Axe," soldiers of the 1/32nd Infantry Regiment often carried equipment weighing nearly one hundred pounds. The soldiers maneuvered up and down the mountains as they moved

U.S. Army First Sergeant David W. Christopher and Staff Sgt. Gordon M. Campbell stand by after setting fire to a Taliban shelter along the Pakistan-Afghanistan border on March 30, 2007. Members of Task Force Fury were patrolling the area during Operation Cat Fury, conducted in Afghanistan. *Spc. Matthew Leary*

from one strategic point to another. During this two-week operation, the infantrymen ensured that the insurgents could not seek refuge in the remote villages. Although they had deployed for months, the soldiers took on the task with the enthusiasm and motivation of freshly deployed mountain soldiers.

Staff Sergeant Matthew Guyatte, a squad leader in 3rd Platoon, explained, "It boils down to intestinal fortitude. I think a lot of people couldn't go up and down these ridges. It's not just once a week, sometimes it's two or three times a day. It takes a lot of will to accomplish these missions. The motivation behind these battle-hardened soldiers varies but only to a small degree. For the most part, they refuse to disappoint their comrades and families by not doing their part."

Elaborating on the motivation of this brotherhood, Spc. Robert Mojarro said, "If I don't make it up that hill, my squad is down an automatic weapon and they have less firepower to suppress and kill the enemy." Reinforcing these comments, Spc. Vincent Kastner said, "You don't want to let the team down. You can't let the leadership down. We have a lot of respect for them and I know they respect us a lot. You just do your part and make it home alive."

The soldiers of the 1/32nd Infantry Regiment called "Vikings" made the best of the austere environment during missions. Specialist Robert Robinson, one of the platoon's team leaders, joked. "In the states you can call the Humvee and they'll come pick you up, but here you're eight thousand feet up and you have nowhere to go. You have to make it up the mountain. Seriously, it's family out here; this is all you have until you get home, and you can't let them down." The idea of being stranded in the mountains of Afghanistan is far from their minds.

A soldier from the 162nd Field Artillery Regiment pulls security at the Bara border checkpoint in the Gorbuz District of Khowst Province, Afghanistan. As part of the International Security Assistance Force, he is able to provide security for the area. The soldier is armed with an M16 and mans a M240 7.62mm machine gun. *U.S. Army photo*

Their primary concern for these infantrymen is with one another, their fellow soldiers.

Private First Class John Dora Jr. said, "It's definitely a brotherhood. We're friends for life. My neighbor told me, 'The people you meet in the service are your friends for life,' and it's true. You get through this together. You rely on the person next to you. It's about pride too. I can say I walked the mountains of Afghanistan. We've been through stuff that not a lot people can say 'Hey, I did that.' "

In the end, the soldiers say the biggest way the deployment has changed them is by making them aware of the smaller things in life. Private First Class Justin Hall explained, "It's definitely changed me. It has made me appreciate the smaller things in life everybody back home takes for granted. That's the biggest thing I've gotten from this deployment."

Beyond the bond, pride, and lessons learned, 3rd Platoon soldiers can say they had a successful impact on the mission. The platoon has discovered more than twenty caches and left the insurgents with few places to hide. "If you go out into the Pech Valley and Kunar province, there is a huge difference because of what we've done," added Specialist Robinson.

Task Force Fury Interdicts Terrorists

The soldiers of Task Force Fury headed out from FOB Bermel, Afghanistan, to conduct a five-day mission from March 29 to April 2, 2007. With the support of the ANA, the purpose of Operation Cat Fury was directed at interdicting the movement of enemy force and munitions into Afghanistan.

Soldiers from 2nd Battalion, 87th Infantry Regiment, 3rd BCT, 10th Mountain Division, led the endeavor, setting up vehicle checkpoints, conducting dismounted patrols along mountain ridgelines, and destroying enemy shelters.

According to Capt. Jason Dye, commander of Company B, 2/87th Infantry Regiment, "The purpose of Operation Cat Fury was to get back into the areas the enemy has historically operated. We wanted to get a head start on this operational season."

Staff Sergeant Jeffrey Hall, a squad leader with Company B, added, "The soldiers of 2/87th Infantry Regiment were well versed with the operational area,

Private First Class Joshua Correia, of Company D, 2nd Battalion, 87th Infantry Regiment, 10th Mountain Division, scans his sector during a night patrol for enemy movement near the Pakistan border in Paktika province, Afghanistan. *Spc. Bem Minor*

having spent the past fourteen months in Afghanistan, a factor that increases their proficiency in conducting operations like this. . . . Although soldiers conducted numerous vehicle checkpoints, a large portion of the mission consisted of dismounted patrols. You've got to have people on the ground walking the area. Your objective cannot be completed without ground forces." Taking the time to search these remote areas is crucial during missions.

Their mission required the infantrymen to climb the steep mountainous terrain akin to those mountain soldiers who scaled the cliffs at Riva Ridge. Captain Dye recounts, "The terrain is deceptive. It doesn't look too bad, but the area is large, mountainous, and inhospitable. In one area, inaccessible to vehicles along the border, multiple rudimentary living structures were discovered and subsequently destroyed. Shelters such as these were used by enemy fighters to camouflage themselves from aircraft, Afghan National Security Force elements, and International Security Assistance Forces. The assistance of the ANA during the operation was a benefit to both militaries. Using them in our operation gives us additional combat power and gives them an opportunity to work side-by-side with us and increase their military professionalism. Also, with their familiarity of the area, the ANA is capable of noticing elements of the terrain that are out of place or simply do not look right. This type of information can be crucial during combat operations. Although no significant enemy activity was discovered, the mission allowed the

An example of a playing card used by 10th Mountain Division soldiers to better acquaint themselves with Iraq's landmarks. One of the purposes of the cards is to prevent unwarranted damages to these ancient locations. *U.S. Army photo*

Lieutenant Colonel Mark Odom, commander, 1st Squadron, 40th Cavalry Regiment, 4th BCT (Airborne), 25th Infantry Division, discusses upcoming actions with leaders from 2nd BCT, 10th Mountain Division, at a patrol base south of Baghdad. Insurgents attacked the patrol base but were quickly repelled by paratroopers and soldiers from 1/40th Cavalry and 2/10th Mountain. *Command Sgt. Maj. Norman Corbett*

troops to establish their presence in the area and deter future activity. The border areas have traditionally been areas that terrorists operate out of."

Operation Iraqi Freedom

"Shock and Awe" began on March 20, 2003, just past 0530 hours local time in Baghdad, Iraq. The morning quiet was supplanted by the sound of explosions as smart bombs and cruise missiles from U.S. and coalition forces rained down on the city. Operation Iraqi Freedom (OIF) and the liberation of the Iraqi people had begun. Although the invasion of Iraq was accomplished in a matter of weeks, the subsequent transformation from a dictatorship to a democracy has taken substantially longer.

1st Brigade Combat Team

On August 12, 2005, after a year of refitting and training, soldiers of the 1st Battalion, 87th Infantry (Task Force Summit), deployed to Camp Liberty, Iraq, in support of OIF. The soldiers of the task force operated in western Baghdad, which encompassed the districts of Shulla, Khadra, Amariyia, Bakaria, and Ghazaylia—a highly complex area consisting of dense urban terrain populated by more than eight hundred thousand Iraqi citizens jam-packed in less than thirty square kilometers.

The task force conducted combat and humanitarian operations specifically targeting the heart of the insurgency in Baghdad. Such missions significantly reduced the number of attacks by one-half within the first four months of operations. In addition to conducting training and combined operations with an IA battalion, Task Force Summit ensured the defense of one of the most strategic sites in Iraq, the Abu Ghraib Internment Facility. The 1st Battalion, 87th Infantry, facilitated the Iraqi Constitutional referendum in October 2005 and the Iraqi National Election in December of the same year. The task force provided security, which resulted in the seating of the first democratically elected Iraqi government in fifty years.

Corporal Clayton Carroll, from the 10th Mountain Division, patrols Martyrs Market in Baghdad. Armed with a 12-guage shotgun, he is part of Operation Enforcing the Law in Iraq. This mission was in support of the troop surge into Iraq in 2007. *Command Sgt. Maj. Anthony Mahoney*

After a year of highly successful combat operations in western Baghdad, Task Force Summit returned home to Fort Drum, New York, in August 2006.

2nd Brigade Combat Team

In the spring of 2003, the 2/14th Infantry and two companies from 4/31st Infantry deployed to the Central Command (CENTCOM) area of operations (AO) in support of Operations Iraqi Freedom and Enduring Freedom. While these soldiers deployed to southwest Asia, the 2nd Battalion, 87th Infantry, deployed to Fort Knox, Kentucky, in support of the Stryker Initial Operational Test and Evaluation, an exercise that was part of the army's transformation.

The 2nd BCT redeployed in support of OIF. The specially tailored brigade would be augmented with the 1/41st Infantry (mechanized) from Fort Riley, Kansas; 1st Battalion, 509th Infantry Regiment and 58th Combat Engineer Company, opposition force units from Fort Polk, Louisiana, and Fort Irwin, California; 463rd Military Police Platoon from Fort Leonard Wood, Missouri; and Company B, 17th Engineers, from Fort Bragg, North Carolina. The collection of units gathered together in Kuwait and made the four-day ground assault into Baghdad in July 2004.

The commando brigade initially secured the Baghdad International Airport area to the southwest of the Iraqi capital. These actions successfully protected the military and civilian air traffic from rocket, mortar, and shoulder-fired antiaircraft weapons and allowed the airport to be opened to civilian traffic in August 2004.

In October 2004, the commando brigade took over control of the entire sector of western Baghdad, including the districts of Abu Ghraib, Monsour, Khadamiyah, and the notorious "Route Irish," the highway running from the Baghdad Airport to the International Zone. The 2nd BCT, 1st Cavalry Division ("Blackjack Brigade"), took several retransmission elements from Company B, 10th Signal Battalion, for the duration of the fight. The commandos likewise accepted temporary command and control of 2/12th Armored, 2/7th Cavalry, 1/5th Infantry, 2/82nd Field Artillery, 91st Engineers, 4/5th ADA, a platoon of

U.S. Army soldiers from Company C, 2nd Battalion, 22nd Infantry Regiment, 1st BCT, 10th Mountain Division, and IA soldiers arrive by air assault to search villages through ten miles of terrain prohibited to vehicles along the Zaghytun Chay River, about fifty miles southeast of Kirkuk, Iraq. *Staff Sgt. Samuel Bendet*

A soldier of the 10th Mountain Division provides security for his platoon as they search a nearby mosque. He is armed with an M4 carbine and has attached an Aimpoint sight and AN/PEQ-4 laser sight. *Courtesy 10th Mountain Division PAO*

Estonian infantry, 127th Military Police Company, and the 303rd IA Battalion (later redesignated 2nd Battalion, 1st Brigade, 6th IA Division).

In the fall of 2004, insurgent activity increased in Sadr City, which resulted in the movement of 1/41st Infantry and Company B, 2/14th Infantry, to support 1st BCT, 1st Cavalry, against the Mahdi Militia in eastern Baghdad, returning to 2/10th Mountain Division (Light Infantry) in February 2005.

The high point of the deployment for the soldiers of the commando brigade was the successful security of the first Iraqi democratic election on January 30, 2006. Security was one of the foremost concerns for the election. It is estimated 60 percent of the citizens in the western area of Baghdad, which the 2nd BCT, 10th Mountain Division, was responsible for, voted in the election. Throughout the country seven million Iraqis would vote during this landmark election. In the 2nd BCT, 10th Mountain Division AO, some of the citizens in Baghdad walked almost twenty kilometers to place their ballots.

During the election the insurgents made attempts to frighten off or kill those citizens trying to cast their votes. Out of nine suicide bombers in Iraq on election day, five were in the 2nd BCT's AO. Fortunately, none of these had any effect on the determination of the Iraqi people. Operation Commando Freeze was a tactical victory for the 2nd BCT and a strategic defeat for the insurgency. In addition to providing security for the election, the soldiers of the 2nd BCT detained 745 insurgents.

After years of oppression under Saddam Hussein, the Shia majority gained political power and the Sunni minority lost their political status. This created the potential for an attack against the holiest Shia celebration of Ashura (a Muslim holiday). The possibility for such an attack was assessed as high, and the soldiers of the BCT carried out the task of defending the Khadamiyah Shrine with the 303rd IA Battalion and the Amarah Battalion. The efforts of the BCT resulted in a successful and peaceful holiday for the Shia pilgrims.

In February 2005, Company C, 2/14th Infantry, and Company B, 4/31st Infantry, reunited with their parent battalions in Iraq. Without any delay these two companies began to conduct operations in Baghdad with Company C, 2/14th, operating in eastern Abu Ghraib and Company B, 4/31st, in Khadamiyah.

During the spring of 2005, the 2nd BCT conducted area security operations to protect and secure the Shia Muslims making the Arba'een pilgrimage. This Muslim holiday, observed by nearly five hundred thousand pilgrims, memorialized the carrying of Imam Hussain's martyred body from his execution site in Khadamiyah to the holy site in Najaf. Once again due to the diligence and respect of the 2nd BCT's soldiers, the event was conducted with minimal interference by the insurgents.

As the newly elected Iraqi government began to evolve and the governing council began to form, the 2nd BCT secured passage of the elected officials and government leaders to the International Zone to participate in what was known as the "seating" of the Transitional National Assembly. This was a repetitive mission, executed every two to three days as the government began to meet more regularly.

In April 2005, the 2nd BCT began a relocation task as part of the integration plan for the 48th BCT, Georgia Army National Guard, and redeployment of the 2nd BCT, 10th Mountain Division. The plan would conduct a series of relieving units in place and transferring battle space with the 256th BCT, Louisiana Army National Guard, swapping the western area of urban Baghdad with the western and southern rural regions once again.

U.S. Army Soldiers from Battery A, 2nd Battalion, 15th Field Artillery Regiment, 10th Mountain Division (Light Infantry), along with IA soldiers, conduct a foot patrol through an area that has been frequented with attacks on coalition forces. *Sgt. Jacob Smith*

The initial moves allowed the 2nd BCT to assume all of Abu Ghraib, including the external security of the Abu Ghraib Internment Facility and the Aqurquf area to the north of Abu Ghraib. The 2nd BCT's forces were arranged as follows: Task Force 2/14th retained eastern Abu Ghraib, Task Force 1/41st assumed western Abu Ghraib, Task Force 4/31st assumed the prison security mission, and Task Force 2/15th assumed the northern area. During this time the BCT accepted the 3rd Muthana Brigade, 6th IA Division, and conducted Operation Brickyard (later renamed Commando Squeeze Play in line with 3rd Infantry Division operational naming convention). During this operation the BCT supported the 3/6th IA's detention of more than 440 insurgents, bringing attacks in Abu Ghraib down from twenty per day to only two or three per day.

Task Force 1/41st and 4/31st conducted battle handovers of western Abu Ghraib with 1/11th Armored Cavalry Regiment (ACR) on June 1, 2005, and the BCT began to focus on an operation in southern Baghdad called Operation Commando Squeeze Play South. The BCT took over the responsibility in the Mamudiya, Yuosafiya, and Latifiya areas south of Baghdad in late May 2005. The BCT also assumed tactical control of the 1st Brigade, Iraqi Intervention Force; 4th Brigade, 6th IA Division; 4th Public Order Brigade; and 2nd Brigade Ministry of Interior Commandos. Operation Commando Squeeze Play South commenced on June 2, 2005. Upon completion on June 3, 2005, the BCT, along with Iraqi security forces, had detained 366 insurgents. Additionally, as seen in Abu Ghraib, attacks diminished from thirty per day prior to the operation to two or three per day.

Upon completion of Operation Commando Squeeze Play South, the soldiers of the 2nd BCT refocused their attention on the integration of the 48th BCT to assume operations west of Baghdad. Units and staff sections of the brigade conducted relief-in-place tasks and trained

Soldiers from 2nd Battalion, 15th Field Artillery Regiment, 2nd BCT, 10th Mountain Division, and Iraqi soldiers from the 4th Brigade, 6th IA Division, search for terrorists and their weapons in Mahmudiyah. The tall native grasses make good hiding places for weapons. *Staff Sgt. Bennie Corbett*

for the 48th to assume the AO with the final transfer of authority between the brigades on June 17, 2005.

On June 21, 2005, the 2nd BCT, 10th Mountain Division headquarters departed Iraq. During their tour of duty, the commando's area of responsibility of western Baghdad suffered the highest concentration of casualties in Iraq and had the largest number of enemy contacts. Throughout their deployment the 2nd BCT conducted more than 66,000 combat patrols; captured 1,905 detainees; came under 645 IED attacks; discovered 413 IEDs; endured 316 mortar attacks, 148 rocket attacks, 65 indirect fire attacks of undetermined type, 537 small-arms fire attacks, 128 rocket propelled grenade attacks, 136 coordinated attacks, 14 surface-to-air missile attacks, 165 attacks against local nationals, and 7 suicide bomber attacks; detonated 56 vehicle-borne IEDs (VCIED); detonated 21 vehicles that carried IEDs; detonated 3 VCIEDs; and discovered another 4 VCIEDs.

Although the 10th Mountain Division conducted mostly combat operations, the division also conducted civil affairs missions. The 2nd BCT civil-military operations team, which consisted of a civil-military operations officer, brigade engineer cell, and project management team, was active in three of the lines of operation: governance, essential services, and economic development. Active in the local government, the 2nd BCT worked closely with neighborhood and district councils to strengthen ties with the local populace and improve the function of the local government.

The 2nd BCT repaired critical infrastructure in western Baghdad in the Districts of Kadhimiya, Al Mansour and Abu Ghraib, as well as in the rural areas of Saba Al Bor and Mahmudiya. Their main civil affairs activities focused on the essential areas of sewer, water, electricity, and trash removal. The 2nd BCT conducted more than three hundred civil-military operations projects.

Specialist Olli Toukolehto and Pfc. Michelle Winicki, both of Company C, 2nd Battalion, 10th Infantry Regiment, Brigade Support Detachment, 10th Mountain Division, fill prescriptions for Iraqi local nationals during a combined medical assistance mission with the IA near Mahmudiyah, Iraq. *Sgt. Martin Newton*

In addition, the project management team monitored another seventy-one projects funded by external organizations. These projects would prove to be critical factors in improving essential services for more than three million Iraqis. A key area of economic development that the 2nd BCT focused on in the rural areas was the improvement of the agricultural industry. The brigade delivered more than three hundred tons of wheat and barley seed, more than one hundred tons of fertilizer, in excess of thirty water pumps, and twenty generators for rural power development to enhance essential water availability for irrigation.

Crucial to the success of these civil affairs missions carried out by the 2nd BCT were efforts led by the 210th FSB. The soldiers of the 210th FSB worked unendingly to provide combat service support, combat health support, and field services to the commando brigade and attached units. The 210th FSB would support eight battalion task forces and brigade troops for the majority of their deployment. This was a major undertaking, since the FSB was designed and resourced to support only four.

One of the greatest achievements of the BCT was the development of the 303rd IA Battalion and the 3rd Muthana Brigade, 6th IA Division. The 303rd, later renamed 2/1/6 IA, could originally execute operations only on a squad and platoon level. As they grew in experience, they developed into a competent, battle-hardened battalion that was feared by the enemy. Soldiers of the 2/1/6 IA conducted hundreds of patrols throughout Ameriya, which was well known for anti-Iraqi forces (AIF) operations and cells. The men of the 2/1/6 IA conducted missions that resulted in the rounding up of dozens of AIF planners, facilitators, and operators. In due course the 2/1/6 IA was assigned to defend Haifa Street, a road made infamous by the QJBR and Ansar al Sunna terror cell attacks. Within a matter of weeks, 2/1/6 had regained the street, bringing stability to the area. The QJBR is the Organization of Jihad's Base in the Country of the Two Rivers, led by Abu Musab al-Zarqawi.

U.S. Army soldiers from the 2nd Battalion, 15th Field Artillery Regiment, 2nd BCT, 10th Mountain Division, and IA soldiers from the 1st Battalion, 4th Brigade, 6th IA Division, patrol a rural village in Mahmudiyah, Iraq. *Staff Sgt. Bennie Corbett*

A soldier from the 2nd Brigade, 10th Mountain Division, compiles a list of captured weapons from a search conducted of the Al Abass Mosque in western Baghdad. *Senior Airman Lapedra Tolson*

The second achievement was the 3rd Muthana Brigade's occupation of FOB Constitution in the heart of Abu Ghraib. Again, the introduction of a competent, disciplined unit brought stability to an area high in enemy contact. These accomplishments were made possible by the Commando Advisory Group.

Twenty-nine commandos made the ultimate sacrifice in support of OIF. By the efforts of the 2nd BCT, twenty-seven million Iraqis now have a democratically elected government.

Upon return to Fort Drum, the 2nd BCT began transformation into the new brigade structure, drawing new equipment and developing new capabilities unique to the transformed infantry BCT. Added to the BCT were 2/71st Cavalry (later reflagged to 1/89th Cavalry), 2nd Brigade Special Troops Battalion, and reflagging the FSB to 210th Brigade Support Battalion.

In March and April, the BCT conducted a six-week National Training Center rotation in Fort Irwin, California, fighting the opposition force and developing experience in full-spectrum operations to include lethal, nonlethal, civil-military, and information operations.

Currently, the Commando BCT is deployed in support of combat operations in support of the GWOT.

2nd Brigade Combat Team Works with Iraqi Army Troops

Operation Wolverine Alesia was a joint operation designed to deny terrorists sanctuary along Route Tampa, the military designation for Iraqi Highway One, leading into Baghdad from the south. The operation was named for a Roman battle that was led by Julius Caesar against the Gauls in 52 B.C. At the fortifications of Alesia, Caesar's army surrounded the enemy, defeating them with siege warfare. Working together with the IA and MultiNational Division Baghdad, Iraqi troops and the mountain soldiers uncovered the largest cache in the history of the brigade.

Acting on a tip from a local resident, soldiers from 3rd Battalion, 4th Brigade, 6th IA Division, and Troop B, 1st Squadron, 89th Cavalry Regiment ("Wolverines"), 2nd BCT, 10th Mountain Division, uncovered the cache while conducting Operation Wolverine Alesia near Yusufiyah, Iraq, just ten miles southwest of Baghdad. The area around Yusufiyah had long been identified as a safe haven for al Qaeda and former regime forces. It was reported that numerous insurgent attacks originated from this area against Baghdad and coalition and Iraqi security forces.

As the soldiers dug deeper and deeper into the earth, they continued to discover more of the mortar ammunition.

U.S. Army soldiers from Battery A, 2nd Battalion, 15th Artillery Regiment, 2nd BCT, 10th Mountain Division, discuss movement during a combined mission with the IA in Lutafiyah, Iraq. *Sgt. Martin Newton*

The cache site was located near the main highway, called Route Tampa, which led to the Iraqi capital. The substantial weapons cache included an excess of 1,100 81mm HE mortar rounds. Such an extensive find would assuredly have an effect on the insurgents' offensive operations. During the operation the IA soldiers also detained four individuals for suspicious activity in the vicinity of the cache.

According to Lt. Col. Mark Suich, the 1/89th's commander, "These mortar rounds are in the configuration to use as improvised explosive devices [IEDs]. The mortar rounds in this state cannot be used for indirect fire; they are fabricated and stored to be used against the coalition and sectarian enemies as IEDs. We put a significant reduction in the enemy's ability to emplace IEDs in this area today. We are pretty sure that these are affiliated with al Qaeda in Iraq."

Major Mark Aitken, executive officer of the 1/89th, related, "This is what we refer to as a weapons supermarket-type cache. The terrorists place a large cache of weapons in one place to draw from. They then preposition what they draw in many other smaller caches around the countryside."

Operation Wolverine Alesia was indeed operating under a lucky star, because a second cache was located near the first. Soldiers from Company C, 1/89th, located twenty 120mm mortar rounds, twenty-six 81mm mortar rounds, four medium machine guns, eight thousand rounds of machine-gun ammunition, three rifle scopes, sixty fragmentation hand grenades, fifty pounds of improvised explosives, twenty-seven boxes of 5.56mm rifle ammunition, and ten rocket-propelled grenade projectiles. An explosive ordnance disposal team was

Specialist Clifford Flint (right), who serves as a cavalry scout with the 1st Squadron, 89th Cavalry Regiment, 2nd BCT, 10th Mountain Division, assists an Iraqi soldier (left) from the 4th Brigade, 6th IA Division, with marksmanship skills in Baghdad. *Master Sgt. Dave Larsen*

called in to destroy the significant find. It is reported that the explosion could be heard more than twenty miles away.

Major Web Wright, spokesman for the commando brigade remarked, "Today we took more than 1,100 IEDs off the streets of Baghdad. Not only did we take these weapons off the streets, 3/4/6 IA is fully integrated into this operation. Last night, they found three caches and were actively involved in finding these two."

"Polar Bears" Battle Insurgents in Iraq

Infantrymen from the 4th Battalion, 31st Infantry Regiment ("Polar Bears"), 2nd BCT, 10th Mountain Division, used air, land, and water to thwart insurgents from escaping Quarghuli, Iraq. Founded by Saddam Hussein before his fall from power, Quarghuli was one of the richest communities in Iraq. For this reason the village attracted and offered insurgents a safe haven. During prior missions in this area, ofttimes the insurgents managed to escape via the Euphrates River.

During Operation Polar Valor, the soldiers of the 2nd BCT used a coordinated battle plan to stop the insurgents. According to Maj. Robert Griggs, the operations officer (S-3) for 4th Battalion, 31st Infantry, "In the past no one has used boats to go into the village. We used boats to travel down the Euphrates in order to seal off any escape routes that the terrorists may use. We try to pick days that the enemy knows are holidays to the Americans. It is during those times that the enemy is less likely to think we are going to do anything. In the past the units have used helicopters and trucks to get into villages. This is the first time the 2nd BCT has used boats in combat operations. The boats give us another way to get into the village. The boats allowed us to seal off any area that the terrorists may have tried to use to escape."

As soldiers from the Company A, 4/31st Military Transition Team (MiTT) and scouts traveled down the river, soldiers from Company C carried out an air assault from Yusufiyah, Iraq, into the village. As the two companies were diverging on the enemy, the infantrymen from Company D worked with the engineers to clear a road from one strongpoint in the village to their link-up location with the other companies. The objective of the mission was for all of the companies to link up and

Weapons and bomb-making materials were found in the Al Abass Mosque in western Baghdad. Multinational forces continue to conduct operations against targeted insurgent cells prior to the Iraqi national elections in Baghdad. *Senior Airman Lapedra Tolson*

establish a strongpoint within the village, stopping the insurgents from escaping.

Iraqi soldiers from the 4th Battalion, 4th Brigade, 6th IA Division, would also participate in the operation and demonstrate their capabilities. U.S. Army Sergeant First Class Dell Rodriguez, the MiTT sergeant, commented, "The IA soldiers did well. They did everything the right way the first time. They have been doing fairly well in everything and are eager to learn."

One of the IA soldiers, Lt. Hesham, remarked, "The mission was great. It is good that we are clearing a dangerous area from terrorists."

Once the three companies had linked up, they set up temporary battle positions until they could establish a strongpoint in the village. Through hard work, careful planning, and continuous communication, the task of bringing the boats and helicopters together at the same time was successful. According to the plan, the noise of the incoming helicopters served to mask the sound of the boats arriving at the identical moment. One of the local Iraqis stated that he did realize the U.S. soldiers were coming into the village by boats because all he heard were helicopters.

During the operation there was not one insurgent who was allowed to escape the village. The comprehensive planning and execution of a mission by the combined U.S. Army and IA soldiers had eliminated Quarghuli as a safe haven for insurgents. Command Sergeant Major Alexander Jiminez, the 4/31st's senior noncommissioned officer, said, "The soldiers did a fantastic job. They cleared an area, found a suitable place to maintain and find some stability, and established a strongpoint."

Operation Northern Lights

This was a joint U.S. Army and IA operation to locate and destroy insurgent weapons caches. Fielding nearly 1,500 soldiers, the operation included the 3rd Brigade, 6th IA Division, and 1st Battalion, 1st Marine Regiment, moving to blocking positions by ground in front of soldiers from the 2nd Battalion, 22nd Infantry Regiment, 1st BCT, 10th Mountain Division. The soldiers were air assaulted onto the objective in the Abu Ghraib area just west of Baghdad, Iraq, to conduct a cordon and search.

During the mission, soldiers from the 6th IA Division uncovered five weapons caches. Items found in these caches included a machine gun, an RPG rocket launcher, three AK-47 assault rifles, 2,200 PKC machine-gun rounds, two boxes of gunpowder, an Iraqi police jacket, eighteen 106mm tank rounds, four hundred blasting caps, forty artillery rounds, seventeen pressure plate initiators, twenty Motorola radio initiators, and

Pictured are the contents of multiple caches that were discovered in a cemetery by soldiers of the 2nd Battalion, 15th Infantry Regiment, 2nd BCT, 10th Mountain Division, and the 4th Brigade, 6th IA Division, during Operation Eagle Chancellorsville. *Sgt. 1st Class Angela McKinziev*

thousands of .50-caliber machine gun rounds. They would also detain a suspected insurgent near one of the caches. Operations of this type were based on intelligence, including tips from local Iraqis. Concerned citizens would report that the IA insurgents had been working in an area and were stockpiling IED-making materials to prepare for future attacks in Baghdad.

Operation Eagle Chancellorsville

Operating in the Said Abdulla Corridor in Iraq, soldiers from the 10th Mountain Division and IA forces have been working closely with the local populace to rid the area of al Qaeda. Acting on a tip from the locals, the soldiers from the 2nd Battalion, 15th Field Artillery Regiment (FAR), 2nd BCT, 10th Mountain Division, and the 4th Brigade, 6th IA Division, embarked on their mission. Their task was to deny the enemy a safe haven from which to conduct their attacks against U.S., coalition, and Iraqi forces in the 2/15th field artillery's AO.

According to 1st Lt. Dave Kendzior, a platoon leader with the 2/15th FAR, "The local population has pledged its support by moving alongside IA and U.S.

U.S. Army Second Lieutenant Andrew Archer, Delta Company, 2nd Battalion, 22nd Infantry Regiment, 1st BCT, 10th Mountain Division, looks inside a building at the Citadel in Kirkuk, Iraq. *Staff Sgt. Dallas Edwards*

forces. They have been instrumental in leading us to caches and buildings that al Qaeda have been hiding in. Concerned citizens have not only led us to caches, but to members of al Qaeda.Because of the true partnership between 2/15th FAR and 4/6th IA disrupting al Qaeda in the area, we have forced them to find refuge somewhere else."

The purpose of the operation was to deny a safe haven to the enemy within the 2/15th FAR AO. As other operations conducted by sister units of the 10th, this operation yielded several caches including those hidden in cemeteries. A major find included twelve rocket-propelled grenade rounds, a 152mm artillery round, an IED, three PKC machine guns, two AK-47 assault rifles, a Dragonov sniper rife with a scope, four RPG launchers, five mortar sights, seventy mortar primers, twenty mortar charges, a 60mm mortar round, a camera flash IED initiator, three IA uniforms, three Kevlar helmets, eleven mortar fuses, nineteen RPG boosters, two bolt cutters, an aid bag, a handheld radio charger, three Global Positioning Systems, thirty-three thousand rounds of PKC ammunition, various IED components, a roll of copper wire, and two ammunition vests. Of significant importance was the finding of the IA uniforms. Using the bogus uniforms, members of al Qaeda would impersonate the soldiers, allowing them to move about with impunity.

Captain Blake Keil, a battery commander with 2/15th FAR, commented, "In our area we have noticed an increase in the local populace's willingness to assist coalition forces in ridding the area of al Qaeda."

As the United States continues to prosecute the GWOT against Islamofascism around the globe, the soldiers of the 10th Mountain Division will answer the call. In spite of the odds or hardships, the men and women of the 10th Mountain Division will bring terrorists to justice or justice to them. Steeped in the heritage of those mountain soldiers of World War II, the infantrymen of the 10th continue their "climb to glory."

Acknowledgments

First, I acknowledge God; may He continue to hold our great country and those who defend it, in the hollow of His hand. My thanks to Steve Gansen—editor, Zenith Press; Harry Sarles, Caroline Bernabei, U.S. Army Public Affairs, New York; Benjamin Abel, Public Affairs, Fort Drum, NY; Harry Coleman, Charlie Hunt, John Imbrie, Thomas Brooks, 10th Mountain Division Association; Chris McGurk, Iraq-Afghanistan Veteran's Association; Wendy Schrupp, NSP; Dennis Hagen, Coi E. Drummond-Gehrig, Denver Public Library; U.S. Army Institute of Heraldry; and Digital Video and Imagery Distribution System Images, reports and assorted interviews: Spc. Matthew Leary, Task Force Fury Public Affairs; Capt. Scott M Betts, 101st Combat Aviation Brigade Public Affairs; Sgt. 1st Class Thomas Mills, Sgt. Amber Robinson, Task Force Spartan Public Affairs; Staff Sgt. George Beckett, Company C, 3rd Squadron, 71st Cavalry, 10th Mountain Division; Pfc. Aubree Rundle, Task Force Pegasus Public Affairs; Army Spc. Matthew Leary, Task Force Fury Public Affairs; Spc. Jon H. Arguello, 22nd Mobile Public Affairs Detachment, 2nd BCT, 10th Mountain Division Public Affairs; Maj. Webster Wright, Staff Sgt. Angela McKinzie, 2nd BCT, 10th Mountain Division Public Affairs; and Sgt. 1st Class Thomas Mills, Spc. Jason Jordan, Spc. Chris McCann, Defense Visual Information Center.

Glossary

ACOG—advance combat optical gunsight
ACR—armored cavalry regiment
ADA—air defense artillery
AIF—anti-Iraqi forces
ANA—Afghan National Army
AO—area of operation
APC—armored personnel carrier
BAR—Browning automatic rifle
BCT—brigade combat team
BUIS—backup iron sight
CONUS—continental United States
DISCOM—division support command
DoD—Department of Defense
down range—physically located in a combat zone
EBR—enhanced battle rifle
FAR—field artillery unit
FOB—forward operating base
FSB—forward support battalion
GWOT—Global War on Terrorism
HDS—holographic display sight
HEDP—high-explosive, dual-purpose
HE—high-explosive

Glossary (continued)

HMMWV **"Humvee"**—high-mobility multipurpose wheeled vehicle
IA—Iraqi Army
IED—improvised explosive device
IFOR—implementation force
IR—infrared
KFOR—Kosovo force
LAW—light antitank weapon
Ma Deuce—the Browning .50-caliber machine gun; weapon's designation, "M2"
MOUT—military operations on urban terrain
NATO—North Atlantic Treaty Organization
NSP—National Ski Patrol
NVG/NVD—night vision goggles/night vision device
OEF—Operation Enduring Freedom
OIF—Operation Iraqi Freedom
QRF—quick reaction force
RF—reinforcing force
RIS—rail interface system
RPG—rocket-propelled grenade
SASS—semiautomatic sniper system
SFOR6—Stabilization Force Six
SOF—special operations force
SOG—study and observation group
SOPMOD—special operations peculiar modification
SO—special operations
SWS—sniper weapon system
TUAV—tactical unmanned aerial vehicle
VCIED—vehicle-borne improvised explosive device
VLI—visible light illuminator

Index